ALAN SILLITOE'S
NOTTINGHAMSHIRE

══ Alan Sillitoe's ══
NOTTINGHAMSHIRE

Words by
ALAN SILLITOE

Photographs by
DAVID SILLITOE

GRAFTON BOOKS
A Division of the Collins Publishing Group

LONDON GLASGOW
TORONTO SYDNEY AUCKLAND

Grafton Books
A Division of the Collins Publishing Group
8 Grafton Street, London W1X 3LA

Published by Grafton Books 1987

British Library Cataloguing in Publication Data

Sillitoe, Alan
Alan Sillitoe's Nottinghamshire.
1. Nottinghamshire—Description and travel
I. Title
914.25′204858   DA670.N9

ISBN 0–246–12852–6

Typeset in Great Britain by
BAS Printers Limited
Over Wallop, Hampshire
and printed by R. J. Acford, Chichester,
Sussex

CONTENTS

NOTTINGHAM CITY

Suburbs spread from the city centre on all sides. In the old days you went into the middle to look for a job, or to collect your dole, or when you were 'summonsed' to court, or to ask at the rent office for more time to pay off the arrears. Things must be similar today (though without the same kind of privation) because the clockhand has come full circle. The centre and the outskirts have been at odds throughout history.

Before the industrial revolution the old village of Radford on the banks of the Leen was described by Throsby as 'a little paradise'. The river was diverted into channels, and pleasure gardens laid out. A pavilion was built on a slight rise of ground, whose ruin still stood up to a few years ago.

After the middle of the nineteenth century the area between the stream and the city was speedily covered with back-to-back houses, and many of the ordinary terrace type. Not long ago the mangonels and bulldozers of redevelopment came, and for a time the landscape was even flatter than Hiroshima. Many of the old dwellings had clean bricks, and were well pointed. A bathroom above each scullery would have completed their desirability. The streets were neatly cobbled, but when destruction is in the offing there is no holding it back.

An irreplaceable spirit was wiped out, and no one yet realises quite what has disappeared, though the erratic flight of petrol bombs must give some indication.

After the rubble had been cleared only the pubs stood, which was

Wollaton Park

something to be grateful for. The Nottingham Arms, the White Horse and the Dover Castle can still figure on a pub-crawler's list. Hundreds of little houses are gone and, looking across the landscape, one sees how small that zone was which seemed so vast and complicated when covered with streets.

Even when you knew every junction, twitchell and double-entry (this latter not a system of book-keeping, at least not then, but a concealed trackway which, connecting two streets, figured high in the tactics of escape and manoeuvre) you never could tell when a gas lamp glowed that someone in the nearby dark was not using its light as an ambush pen. Neither did you know what waited behind the corner it stood on. But you weren't in danger from more than a stray thump, and you often dealt out the same, giving as good as you got – sometimes more, in case next time you got more than you were able under the circumstances to give. You invented perils, exaggerated pitfalls, occasionally felt that you even called them up. Potholes became foxholes, and foxholes as often as not turned into underground caverns full of guns and ammunition, food and, later, more gold than Monte Cristo ever dreamed of. In such streets you could outdream everybody.

In grown-up life you forget all that. Walking on Ilkeston Road one day a window cleaner came down his ladder and called to me. It was Ted Butler, a man of over forty like myself, and after wiping himself on a piece of rag we shook hands. For years he'd been managing a warehouse, then lost his job when the firm went broke. After six months on the dole he found a ladder, took a bucket and cloth from home, and went around the streets touting for custom, finding enough to get a living. After a while he bought an old banger and better ladders. Contract work came his way, which included the school whose windows he'd been cleaning up to a minute ago.

'I'd never been up a ladder in my life,' he said, 'and it took some getting used to. I'm doing all right now, though.'

We met later for a pint in the Nottingham Arms, and talked about how things were when we were kids. His father had been a postman, and the family seemed like aristocrats to me whose father was on the dole, and whose thirty-eight shillings a week kept two grown-ups and four children, the equivalent of about forty pounds today. Ted's mother often gave me bread and butter and a cup of tea when I called for him.

'On summer evenings,' he said, over the second pint, 'we waited for the lamplighter to come round. Do you remember? We went close, to sneak a look up the length of his arm to see how it was done. He chased us away . . .'

A light was left glowing on each street corner, and an equal light in the dim blue sky tried to outlive it. But the sky grew blacker, and the yellow gas light turned something near to white, and we climbed the lamp post more often in the dark than during the day because at night the gas light seemed to be winning against adversity the longer it glowed, and we felt a desire to get as close as possible. If a grown-up came by we would get down and run away, knowing he or she would shoo us out of it in case we damaged the light. He would even bat our tabs if we chelped him. If it was a woman she would tell us off for risking our limbs, and would threaten to tell our dads if we chelped *her*. Whatever we did was wrong, which we half liked, otherwise life would have been dull, and kids can't stand that. At least we couldn't.

Ted was happy because he had all the work he wanted. 'What more can you want?' he said. His three kids were close to adolescence, and he had recently been rehoused into a 'highrise hencoop'. 'I think they thought they were delousing us rather than rehousing us,' he joked. But he was saving to put the down payment on a house that was no better – but a house all the same – than the dwelling that had been destroyed. 'I don't like my neighbours in the flats. We're on top of each other. Most of them have turned everything into a pigsty. In the old places you might have a pigsty on either side – though I can't remember any except old Bingham the chimney sweep who had nine kids – but at least you could shut your door and know that your own place was all right. And even if they were on either side they weren't over your head and under your feet as well.'

As I grew up, the area to be explored was without limits. Lenton

Maid Marian's Way. Underpass

was contiguous with Radford. My grandfather had been a blacksmith there, and met my grandmother when she was a barmaid at the White Hart. Both grandparents are buried in the nearby churchyard, with their eldest son. Lenton was once more powerful than Nottingham because of the great Cluniac priory, founded in 1155 by William Peveril, who also built the Castle a mile to the east. In 1538 Henry VIII had the prior, eight monks, and four local labourers hanged at the gates because they were suspected of treason, but really because he wanted to get his hands on the priory revenues. The ruins of the foundation have long since vanished.

Other adjoining suburbs were Basford, and the Hyson Green area which is now the red light district of the town, into which I strayed because the cinemas seemed more glamorous, and there was a bigger public library. I went to the Meadows to visit my aunt and cousins, until the whole conurbation became known. A few streets of the Meadows are still there, as well as the kids who go with it. On those houses there is no evidence of vandalism, and no smears of graffiti such as adorn the walls of the Top Valley estate, messages of defiance and melancholy, folk poetry for the edification of passers-by.

Beyond all these suburbs and, eventually, beyond the hundred-mile bike range of the city, there was the world, and I was never aware of having to go through London to get to it, except to use its railway stations as stepping stones.

Spiralling back in time and vision to Nottingham, whenever I saw the words in the indicator-window of a doubledecker bus saying CITY CENTRE I was reminded of that fundamental separation of the two parts, one of which has space for its inheritance, and the other power.

The centre has been cleaned up but not, as in some cities, depersonalised. Even in childhood I was aware of the brash self-confidence of Nottingham, though perhaps the less conscious you are of it the more certain you may be to acquire it. I haven't lived in Nottingham since I was eighteen, and only left it to find out what was beyond, not because I disliked it.

The house I was born in still stands, as does the first school I went to, which is now an electrical goods store. The last school I attended is a community centre. At those schools I received sufficient scholarship to enable me to learn as much as I wanted on my own after I had left, and one can hardly say better than that.

The Raleigh Bicycle Factory, where I went to work at fourteen, nowadays employs two thousand people instead of the eight when in its prime. The once glorious façade of the offices is boarded up, or advertises the presence of smaller firms which are taking it over.

The plywood and jacquard factory has also gone, as has the engineering workshop by a railway embankment in the Meadows owned by Bert Firman, a tolerant and generous employer who worked among us like the rest. The railway line has been torn up as well.

The public libraries are there, but the places that have disappeared include every other house I lived in, and they were many, because our moonlight flits were always one turn of the handcart wheels ahead of the rent man's flat feet. Pawnshops, pubs and cinemas have been flattened, or converted, as if they represented a certain religion that the authorities disagreed with. Whole patterns of streets have been wiped out. Many small houses in which a better life could have been led than in the highrise hencoops, as Ted Butler suggested, were demolished before their time but, as one of the workmen said with quiet Nottingham irony while hoisting himself back into his crane-cabin to destroy another street: 'That's progress, duck!'

A shopping centre has been put up in place of the second railway station. New hotels have been built, but the Flying Horse remains, as does the George Hotel where I sometimes stayed. The second-hand book shops have moved to Mansfield Road, a short distance from the centre. On a dinnertime bike ride from the factory in 1945 I called at Frank Wore's and found a first English edition (1876) of Baedeker's *Palestine and Syria* for sixpence – and took it on my first visit to Israel in 1973.

What does remain is an area in the city centre whose charm I knew little about when young, the old Lace Market of narrow streets and tall early-nineteenth-century warehouses and factories, which at

Goose Fair

one time constituted Nottingham's glory in the world of lace. A start was to be made on its demolishing, but people of good sense prevailed and it is still intact, an almost silent city being taken over by small hosiery firms, nightclubs and studios. A street called Broadway is to me the most impressive of thoroughfares. Even Elizabeth Williamson (in Pevsner's guide book) mentions it favourably, and that must mean something!

That Nottingham is a progressive city can be proved by the new theatre put up in the sixties, to bitter opposition from the Conservatives on the Council – though the piece of sculpture outside seems (to me) like a blast-off gone wrong. The traffic system has not destroyed the centre, and a motorist may find it difficult to get anywhere near Slab Square, so that after many attempts he could well end up slashing his wrists in some lonely lay-by in Sherwood Forest.

Pedestrians, however, are taken care of, except for the razor-slash (or should I say sabre-cut?) of Maid Marian's Way which separates Slab Square from the Castle, so that if ever the Nottingham Lambs seek to burn it down (again) they must run the gauntlet of fast cars, or risk an ambush by the forces of law and order in the underpass.

The Castle has not changed, nor has the Guildhall, which is still the police headquarters. My family are no strangers to that building. My father was taken there, and thence to prison, for non-payment of debt in the early thirties.

I went to the Castle on a school outing when I was eleven. We were shown through the sandstone tunnel leading to Mortimer's Hole, and made foul jokes as we groped our way along, outstretched hands rubbing the walls and trying not to lose touch with the boy in front. The tale goes that in 1330 Roger Mortimer, the Earl of March, was the lover of Queen Isabella, widow of Edward II. Her son, Edward III, instigated a plot to get rid of him, and the conspirators used this secret way to enter their apartments. Mortimer was hanged at Tyburn, and thus ended another bout of argy-bargy at the old Castle.

At the beginning of the Civil War in 1642 Charles I unfurled his standard nearby, on the spot known as Standard Hill. The wind promptly blew it down which was not a good omen, and Colonel Hutchinson soon pushed him and his cavaliers out of the town. Without Nottingham the Royalist cause was lost, even though the war dragged on for four more years.

Wandering around the town on foot I head for the Castle, uphill all the way from Slab Square. There is a statue of Robin Hood outside the walls. Long rehabilitated, he has been made into a perky and elfin figure who wouldn't harm a fly, though he does appear to be drawing his bow on a deer – or he was, until somebody stole his arrow.

It costs nothing to get through the big gateway, perhaps in the hope that the people of Nottingham will never again set it on fire as they did during the 1831 Reform Bill riots, when it belonged to the Duke of Newcastle. He was later given twenty-one thousand pounds in compensation (about half a million in today's money), at which sum he pulled a very sour face. Three rioters were later hanged, though they were no more responsible for the conflagration than hundreds of others.

I spare a thought for the twenty-eight Welsh boys who in 1212 were held hostage in the Castle for the good behaviour of their elders. When word came that they had broken their parole and would not join his cause, the King called the children in from play and told them their fate. The elder boys remained proud and silent, while the younger ones pleaded for mercy, but the King had them all hanged from the walls. Every castle has its catalogue of horror and injustice, but the killing of the Welsh boys was one of the worst that occurred in Nottingham. I like to think – though I suppose I am wrong – that the modern word *John* for privy stems from this incident.

Approached from the gate, the grey sandstone Castle looks through the trees something like the outside of a Piranesi prison with its flat balustraded roof. One can imagine Scarpio gloating inside, and sympathise with the dagger-thrust of Tosca. In the grounds is a bandstand, and close by a statue of Captain Albert Ball VC. I once stood by the topmost parapet and, looking at the southerly view, wrote the following poem:

10

Goose Fair

Clouds play with floodwater,
distorted shekels between grass
enriched by the tips. The city flattens
surrounding land with rubbish;

binoculars ring the distance like a gun:
from a sea of shining slate
churches lift and chimneys lurch,
modern blocks block visions,

the 'Robin Hood Rifles' drilled in fours
practised azimuths on far-off points,
eyes watering at southern hills
a half-day's march away:

'They'll have to swim the bloody Trent,
God-damn their goldfish eyes!'
Musket balls rush, break glass,
make rammel. The Nottingham Lambs

did more damage than a foreign army,
came through twitchells to spark the rafters,
paint pillars with the soot of anarchy.
The Trent flowed in its scarlet coat

too far off to deal with fire:
the Council got our Castle in the end
protected by Captain Albert Ball VC
who thrust into a cloud-heap above Loos

hoping for his forty-second 'kill'.
In school they said: 'You're born
for Captain Albert Ball
to be remembered. Otherwise, he'd die.'

A private soldier became Icarus:
'Dearest Folks, I'm back again

12

in my old hut. My garden's fine.
This morning I went up, attacked five Huns

above the Line. Got one, and forced two down
but had to run, my ammunition gone.
Came back OK. Two hits on my machine.'
Fate mixed him to a concrete man

an angel overlooking
on the lawn of Nottingham's squat fort.
My memory on the terrace
remembers barges on the Leen

each sail a slice of paper, writing
packed in script of tunic-red.
For eighteen years I blocked the view
no push to send me flying.

Another brain shot down in sleep:
rich Master Robin Hood outside the walls
(where he belongs) robs me of time
and does not give it to the poor.

The whimsical statue stood
with hat and Sherwood weapons
till a Nottingham Lamb removed the arrow
(someone later nicked the bow)

then they stole the man himself
and rolled his statue down the hill
one football Saturday
and splashed it in the Trent:

if you see it moving, take it;
if it doesn't move, steal it bit by bit,
but do not let it rest
till Death with its sonic boom

blows the ball of the sun
through every Castle room.

Goose Fair

By the entrance to the museum are busts of famous Notting-hamshire writers – Byron, William and Mary Howitt, Henry Kirke White, Philip James Bailey, and Thomas Miller the novelist and poet (1808–74) whom I've never heard of.

Inside the museum are paintings by Thomas Sandby, whose brother Paul Sandby (both born in Nottingham) was founder of the English School of watercolour painting. In 1746 he was appointed by the Duke of Cumberland as draughtsman to the survey of the Highlands. Laura Knight, and Richard Parkes Bonnington who was born at nearby Arnold, are also represented.

There is a museum of the Sherwood Foresters, as well as exhibitions of pottery, glass and ceramics. While walking into the main picture gallery I heard a voice say: 'Hello, Alan!'

One of the attendants greeted me, a man in his mid-forties, who turned out to be the son of my cousin killed in Libya during the last war, and whom I hadn't seen for years, so we talked for ten minutes about members of the family I had lost track of.

Perhaps the climb, or maybe the time of day, dries the inner organs. If it's the right time, afternoon tea can be had at the Shire Rooms opposite the gate, a tea so big it makes a meal. If the morning is almost over, however, the descent leads to the Trip to Jerusalem built into the rock on which the Castle stands and claiming to be 'the oldest inn in England'. We are told that the Crusaders left there for the Holy Land in 1189 of the common era, though such sanctified brigandage did little good to Jerusalem or its inhabitants, which fact needn't of course detract from the agreeable nature of the pub, since one can hardly hold the medieval publican responsible for the actions of the louts who happened to drink his beer.

The place is often crowded, so another pleasant pub is the Royal Children, on Castle Gate, not to mention Ye Olde Salutation (1240) on St Nicholas Street. Mostly I make for Yates's Wine Lodge which takes me across the biggest market square in England, otherwise known as Slab Square due to the amount of masonry used in its layout in 1928. We used to think its large area was designed against pub-crawlers, in the hope that by the time they crossed to the other side they would have sobered up. Either that, or a good field of fire was needed from the council house in dealing with rioters. Long Row, along the north side of the square, was a notorious stretch of pavement until recent times for the amount of plain whoring that went on.

The downstairs bar in Yates's is so long it reminds me of that old shaggy dog kind of joke that used to go the rounds:

'They're opening a new pub in town!'

Roars of approval, as if the millenium has arrived:

'Hoo-ray!'

'But there's only one bar!'

Shouts of despair, and threats of riot:

'Boo!'

'It's the longest bar in the world!'

'Hoo-ray!'

'There's only one bar man!'

'Boo!'

'But hundreds of bar maids!'

'Hoo-ray!'

'They aren't selling any beer!'

'Boo!'

'Only whisky!'

'Hoo-ray!'

And so on, almost into infinity with a resourceful narrator, though perhaps parliamentary candidates should note the technique.

The place is famous locally for its wines and liquors, and as I sip my pint I read on the wall behind the bar of Full Ruby, Young Tawny, Bismark, Madeira, Old Rainwater, Red Cap Vodka, Highland Malt, White Australian and Nut Brown, as if such names are the cast for a comic opera.

The space on the public side of the bar takes up the large ground floor, with a few tables set between the pillars. You are, in fact, in a kind of cathedral, at least one that most people would prefer. The ceiling goes up like Chartres, or maybe Southwell, and wide stairs lead to another floor. Here, a gallery goes all around, with tables at

Goose Fair

Peace Festival

which people sit and drink, heavily occupied in the evening. Nearest the street a covered veranda overlooks the road, and there's a bar to save you going downstairs for replenishment. On Saturday night the place is crowded, and though it may not be true that Nottingham girls are the prettiest in England (or the world, as some besotted men have said) they are vivid, lively and spectacularly attired as they troop in. Then Yates's comes into its own, the gayest (in the older sense of the word) place in town.

The evening before, when the place was full, I stood in the toilet getting rid of some of the liquid, as were about a dozen other men, all in silence, when a young woman kicked the door open and, saying 'Excuse me!' as she walked behind us, went in to use one of the empty waterclosets because there was a queue in the women's department next door.

At closing time a bit of thumping went on by the exit, between a truculent drinker and one of the bow-tied bouncers. You are expected to behave yourself in Yates's, especially after its recent face-lift.

But at half past eleven in the morning two elderly couples sip drinks at a table, and two more stand by the bar. I've rarely seen the place so sedate, and mentally thank God that appearances deceive.

On Sunday afternoon a Peace Festival takes place on a grassy area close to the Embankment War Memorial. Tents, exhibitions, things to eat and articles to buy. From a stall of secondhand books I choose *The Battle of the Atlantic* for twenty pence. All kinds of causes lay out their pamphlets and posters: Gay Youth, Vegetarians, Lesbian Youth, CND, Victims of Crime, British Israelites, Neighbourhood Labour Parties, Miners' Support Groups – a badge collector's paradise. You can refresh yourself on candy floss or herbal tea, or eat in 'The Day of the Apocalypse Restaurant'. I wonder what they are serving there, but it turns out to be nothing spectacular. All kinds of delicious looking rissoles and veggie-burgers are available. You can even buy a cup of tea, or a programme.

A rainbow-coloured hot-air balloon is inflated by gas burners. Four volunteer enthusiasts pull at mooring ropes to keep it stable, and within half an hour it hovers in full global splendour a few feet off the ground. Basket attached, the crew intend floating it over Nottingham with messages of peace. Being the real thing, it has a Certificate of Airworthiness, and a pukka call-sign clearly painted: G–OCND.

But a wind blows hard. Our fragile craft might get pushed off course and damaged. It might never come back to base, so the mission is scrubbed. The spherical splendour of peace hovers in full stretch thirty feet above the field. One day there'll be time enough to see it go.

Many people applaud the attempt, but most are too preoccupied with other events to notice. This is a peaceful side to Nottingham, and even a couple of Nottingham Lambs are impressed, two tall young men in studded black leather jackets, with Geronimo hairstyle and earrings, the modern version of the city's traditional roughs. They spend at least four minutes looking at a photo-mosaic of bombed-out Hiroshima, wondering how it was done.

A Peace Fair in Nottingham is a new manifestation of its character. Not that the inhabitants are particularly belligerent, though the town has had more than its fair share of riots. In the best book about the city, *Portrait of Nottingham*, Emrys Bryson says: 'Through most of the eighteenth and nineteenth centuries, the characteristic sounds in Nottingham were the noise of jeering crowds, the whine of musket balls, and the smashing of glass.' Not much different, I suppose, to Brixton and Handsworth today, allowing for the invention of petrol, which increases the crackle of flames in the midnight sky.

The last real riot in the City was in 1958. White youths from the suburbs set out to make an affray against coloured people. Young men walking up Salisbury Street called to others who hung back: 'We're goin' downtown to get some black puddings!' They did not achieve their goal. With help from fire service hosepipes they were scattered by the police, which left more bitterness against the firemen than the blacks – or the police, who after all are only Nottingham Lambs in uniform.

20

The Lace Market

Speaks for itself

In their heyday the Nottingham Lambs must have put the Riot Act through many printings. One of their number was William Thompson the pugilist (1811–80), otherwise known as Bendigo, a name which came from his being one of the triplets called Shadrach, Meschach and Abednego, which local parlance soon reduced to Bendigo.

The Nottingham streets of those days were a good training ground for a natural lefthanded slugger, and Bendigo went on to become the champion prize fighter of England. Such were his rough-housing habits that he was 'up' before the magistrates and committed to prison twenty-eight times. At the age of sixty he turned religious, became a revivalist. While preaching he would occasionally put down his Bible, fervently request God's permission (and get it) then go among the crowd to deal in the only way he knew how with hecklers and troublemakers.

When he died, a mile-long procession followed him to his grave, over which was laid the tombstone of a resting lion. The inscription reads: 'In Memory of William Thompson, "Bendigo" of Nottingham, who died 23rd August 1880, aged 69 years –

> In life always brave, fighting like a lion:
> In death like a lamb, tranquil in Zion.'

I drive to Bulwell cemetery where my father and sister are buried. On the way I pass Shipstone's Brewery at Basford, where a huge golden Star of David is implanted in the middle of the handsome clock on the tower.

It's years since I went to the graveyard, and don't know if I'll be able to locate the family plot. No one walks among the hundreds of stones. Maybe it has such an abandoned look because it's Saturday, though everything seems well cared for.

I walk slowly across the whole area, looking neither left nor right, until the gravestone is at my feet. Instinct led me, or the memory of its location resurfaced because I didn't call on it too hard.

Down from Death Hill, on a piece of ground like reconstituted no man's land from the First World War, a trick-cycle club are having their weekly meeting. Scores of kids speed up and down the humps and hollows with courage and dexterity. They are fascinating to watch, and parents find it so as well, their cars lined up on the grass with tailgates open, revealing plentiful supplies and spares inside. At one dusty escarpment the kids fly through the air, and the miracle is that no one comes off or is hurt, though a Red Cross man stands by in case.

To the west of Nottingham, beyond the stark cubist outline of Players Tobacco Warehouse, on a hill between the Derby and Ilkeston roads, stands Wollaton Hall, the noblest mansion in the county. It is often the first place I go to after driving up the Great North Road to the Nottingham conurbation. I park my car and walk around it, and stay an hour before going to see my family or visit other places.

The Hall belonged to the Willoughbys, who owned the estate for three hundred years before that. The family was founded in 1240 by one Ralph Bugge, perhaps originally Bugger, though no relation (I'm sure) to the Fuggers of Augsberg. The last Bugge I met was a motel owner in Albuquerque, New Mexico, who told me that he frequently attended reunions of the Bugges from all over the world.

One of the Willoughbys, Sir Hugh, died in 1554 while leading an expedition to find the north-east route to China and India along the coast of Siberia. Francis Willoughby (1635–72) was a famous naturalist. Wollaton Hall was built by *Sir* Francis Willoughby out of money from numerous coalpits in the area. The earliest coal in the country was dug near Cossall in 1384. Smythson (who also designed Hardwick Hall for Bess of that name) was the architect, and the building was begun in 1580 and finished in the year that the Spanish Armada was repulsed.

The cost of eighty thousand pounds, together with having to provide dowries for his three daughters, put him permanently into debt, and he died twelve years later in London, poor and miserable, shunned by his family.

The monument he left is one of the most magnificent examples of

Captain Albert Ball VC

Royal Concert Hall

Elizabethan architecture in England, and the first building of my childhood that I looked on with awe and pleasure. When the autumn of orange and gold was on the trees, and the lawns heavy with dew, I would almost race up the hill as if unable to believe the vision I saw. Balustrades, pinnacles, balconies and towers overtopped and flanked a vast façade of windows. The building was the colour of cakey sandstone, a light beige for the top floors, with two massive lower storeys somewhat darker.

I may be harping too much on the past, but in my view the greatest mistake a writer can make is to look more to the future than to the past. A writer who poses as a prophet ends by confusing his soul, and confounding the souls of those who are tempted to listen. Art is confirmation, not affirmation.

To enter the place was equally awesome, but I was always delayed by the row of 1812 cannon spaced along the terrace up the flight of steps and pointing over the parapet. No one stopped us straddling them and making as if we were gunners demolishing the approaching suburbs that concealed some mysterious enemy. They are missing today, though two are placed inside the entrance, their barrels well polished. High above a wall thirty-one muskets with fixed bayonets are arranged in a semi-circle like a navigational protractor from a box of drawing instruments.

The natural history museum has full-sized animals poised and glaring, as well as a wonderful range of exhibits, including geological specimens, a complete education for whoever wants to use it. When our city school was closed down at the beginning of the war for fear of air raids we were given classes here, in a style of building that no public school could match.

Soldiers were billeted under canvas in the park, and in one of the ground-floor rooms an enormous table was covered with books that local people had sent for their distraction. Our classroom on an upper floor had mullioned windows which looked over the grounds and the lake. The taste I received for the spiritual headiness induced by large rooms hasn't yet been lost.

In the gardens behind the Hall is a conservatory, built in 1823 by the Sixth Lord Middleton at a cost of eighty thousand pounds, of which fourteen thousand was spent on camellias. On my present visit the place was closed because people had been going in and stealing the covers of the drainage grates with their elegant floral design. But a young pipe-smoking gardener nearby unlocked it and let us enter. The fluted columns supporting the barrel-vaulted metal roof over the walkways were drainpipes in fact. The glass roofing was tinted, enclosing a heating system to stimulate growing conditions in which the plants and bushes from the Atlas Mountains thrive.

A car from Radio Nottingham waits for the Lord Mayor to open the Goose Fair, and people gather by a sort of boxing ring just in from the road. Kids licking toffee apples squabble impatiently because there's still half an hour to go, and it's starting to rain. Typical bloody weather, someone grumbles.

A workman on the platform puts up a construction of two large silver bells, and the excitement of the kids increases. Those closer to adolescence give him a cheer. It's my first time at an Opening.

A score of dignitaries form up on the platform like two separate squads of infantry, presumably Labour and Conservative, a divided family gathered together for the occasion. A stocky man with a few teeth missing and some kind of regalia around his neck looks a bit like a butcher. A priest, also stocky, wears glasses and has short grey hair. He's about fifty-five, and has such a churlish expression that I wouldn't give much for Robin Hood should he fall into his clutches.

More grown-ups arrive among the audience, but allow the children to stay up front. Behind, Soul Sounds on the Super Waltzer are all set to go as soon as the mayor gives permission. Long-haired young men carry rags and oil cans from cog to cog, checking and polishing.

The kids, who know everything before it happens, shout: 'They're here!' as the most dignified of the dignitaries come on stage in feathered hats, cocked hats, top hats, as if to perform *The Pirates of Penzance*. People are laughing, and more police are present, as if imagining that some fanatic might have it in for the Lord Mayor, who looks however as if he can take care of himself. A huge white

Wollaton Hall

After the match

furry goose with a yellow beak sways back and forth above the people's heads.

The men on stage, with maces and lace cuffs and sticks, are like seventeenth-century revenue officers, and I half expect to see a snuff box or brandy flask going round. The Mayor has a stick, and an even fancier medallion. A law figure, with a wig of curly grey hair, also has one, and so has the woman of the party, who steps forward to open the ceremony:

'Good morning, ladies and gentlemen, Lord Mayor, the civic dignitaries, and also the goose who is giving us the eye [laughs and whistles]. It is my duty here this morning to ask the chief executive to read the proclamation to open this year's Goose Fair, and then the Lord Mayor will speak to you. Mr Hammond has been very ill, so we're pleased to welcome him back today.'

Mr Hammond reads from his parchment in a matter-of-fact voice which could turn at any moment into the hectoring of the Riot Act. That thought, however, is a little premature, because the first molotov cocktail has not yet wobbled towards shopfronts or riot shields. In any case, the days when a mayor could safely read the Act from a balcony of the town hall have long since gone. You can't help having such ruminations whenever a Nottingham crowd gathers, though the one I stand among seems out only for enjoyment.

'Goose Fair 1985, whereas several prescriptive rights and franchises are by divers royal charters and letters patent ratified to the citizens of this city, among which a fair is to be yearly held and kept forever on the feast day of St Matthew the Apostle, which fair by an order of the secretary of state, under the Fairs Act of 1873, be held on the first Thursday in the month of October. It shall continue during the two following days and no longer in each year. Now therefore the Right Worshipful the Lord Mayor doth hereby publicly proclaim that the said fair shall be held and kept accordingly on the third fourth and fifth days of October instant, and doth hereby require that all cattle goods wares and merchandises brought hither to be sold shall be exposed to public view and sold in the open fair and not otherwise, and that no horse mare or gelding shall be sold at this fair but which shall be duly vouched for. God save the Queen!'

There is a very ragged cheer to this patriotic exhortation, but I think the audience was taken by surprise at the sudden ending of the speech, which they were beginning to think would go on for ever.

'I'd have thought it would have rated a bit more cheering than that,' Madam Chairman chides.

'Not in Nottingham, missis!'

'Well, anyway, can we ask the Lord Mayor now if he will officially open the Fair. And please, let's make it a grand occasion and clap him and cheer him.'

The Mayor is a youngish man of about forty, with a short, well-trimmed beard. His garb is positively medieval – as I suppose it should be – with a lace ruff around his neck, a gold brocade robe over his shoulders, and a fine feathered hat.

'Madam Chairman, civic dignitaries, Mr Stevens, members of the council, ladies and gentlemen, I am delighted to have the opportunity this morning to perform one of the city's oldest traditions, the opening of the Goose Fair. Each year Goose Fair continues to be well supported by many citizens and other visitors who come from far and near. I know that the showmen look forward to playing their part in contributing to one of the greatest pleasure-fairs held in this country.

'Goose Fair seems to have a magic all of its own, and an attraction for young people and children which I'm sure would be difficult to equal anywhere else. I recall my own childhood in this city when we all looked forward to Goose Fair, and it seems to have lost none of its magic. I was and am still hoping that the weather will stay fine, and it's not quite Goose Fairish, but it's getting a bit that way now. [A reference to the commencing rain.] With those few words may I again say how delighted I am to have the opportunity of performing the official opening this morning, and I would like to thank the other civic dignitaries and members of the council and all of you for being here. I have now great pleasure in ringing the bells which will give out the message that the 1985 Goose Fair is formally opened, and

Inside the Council House

Council House

give out the traditional cry: "I am the Mayor, who favours the fair, for three days only!"'

As he ding-dongs with gusto the hitherto cynical multitude comes up with loud cheers.

'Give it another ring!' a wag shouts.

He's a good sport, and does. In any case, you ignore a Nottingham Lamb at your peril – though it's not that kind of day. Roundabouts on three sides grind into action. The Lord Mayor has first choice, and for him and his cronies everything is free. His entourage suddenly swells to twice the size. Close at hand are the Alpine Express, the Big Wheel, and the Dive Bomber which feels, I am told, as it goes through the air, as if you're about to take a spill from a motorbike, which is probably why I don't see any Leather Cavaliers in the queue.

On the Dodgems – three rides for £1·20 – it stipulates that children must wear safety belts, that there's to be no smoking, that you must stay seated in the cars, and drive one way only – not as much fun as in the old days, when you took your chance.

Between the main attractions you can play Lucky Numbers at Jolly Jim's, while another stall advertises a prize every time, win or lose. If you're peckish you can stroll along Fast Food Avenue and eat hamburgers, bacon butties, chip butties, popcorn, fresh doughnuts, cockles and mussels, whelks, gingernut, brandysnap, corn on the cob and doner kebab. A group of pretty girls walk by with paper dishes of mushy peas and mint sauce. They wear kiss-me-quick hats (or kiss-me-and-squeeze-me) of a black trilby type more stylish than I remember. The smell of fatty hot dogs must travel miles. So must the noise. Vendors Alley sells watches, portraits, brassware and handbags. You can have your fortune told, or put money into a Salvation Army collecting box.

I was here with my sister in 1935 when a battery of the South Nottinghamshire Hussars in full ceremonial dress fired a royal salute for the jubilee of King George V. We had been given sixpence and a day off school, and it was the first time – though not the last – that we heard gunfire. I was astonished and mesmerised as each salvo burst like a thunderclap only a few yards away, but my five-year-old sister screamed till I took her home.

Someone this morning heard on his CB radio that thousands of milk bottles had been stolen from two schools in the area. A Hyson Green milk float had also been hi-jacked – and not for the milk, though I imagine the purloiners' families would knock that back willingly, before washing the containers at the kitchen sink so that another kind of liquid could be put in. A well attended match at Trent Bridge, on the last day of the fair, is bound to spark off a riot. Police walk around by the half dozen, suggesting that they also listen in on CB radios.

On Friday, even before midday, the attractions which instil hilarity and fear, and shake the guts like dice in a cup, are in great demand. A gleaming and polished engine powers the antique hobby horses that circulate with their heads forward as if bounding away from the terrors of hell. There's a grandeur about each sculptured steed prancing to 'The Flight of the Bumble Bee'. It's nearly forty years since I was here, but the time gap is eliminated when I read 'Proud old time riding horses rode by all with joy. James Noyes and Son' on the circling canopy.

By the end of Saturday night we're ankle deep in fag packets, ice-cream cartons and discarded hats. The Cakewalk of old has become the Rock and Roll Ride. The usual goodnatured Nottingham Goose Fair crowd prevails. You see as many black faces as I suppose there would be white at the Notting Hill Carnival, as well as a fair sprinkling of broad women with sway-walking gaits and grim faces.

The day begins clear, and warm for October. Does this mean there'll be a riot? Most people think it's certain, with a glint in their eyes that suggests they won't particularly mind, Nottingham being Nottingham. The joke of the last few days has been that there are only sixty-eight more looting days to Christmas.

The fair at night is a stupendous glitter. Wherever you look – if you can bear to – it's like the broken middle of a stick of spinning seaside rock, different colours scintillating on a white substance. 'She'll be coming round the mountain when she comes . . .' they sing in their gangs.

The crowd is so thick you can hardly move. The senses quail.

Airborne

Lights flash spectacularly in all directions. Noise cuts out speech. Around midnight the flash of the first molotov cocktail in a nearby street goes unnoticed. The riot takes place off stage, and I don't hear of any arrests. Nor is it reported in the press. Nevertheless, thirty shops are looted, and many cars burned out.

It's not as bad as some had feared, or as others had hoped it would be. The Nottingham police are dab hands at nipping riots in the bud. They've been doing it since the Middle Ages (and probably before) in one guise or another. Well, the Castle was burned down in 1832, but *nobody* liked the Duke of Newcastle. As for the modern police, they aren't called Popkess's Lads for nothing, though perhaps they find it worrying that the Nottingham Lambs now have some Black Sheep among them.

EASTWOOD & SHERWOOD

What drives me back on this particular day I do not know, but I pack a rucksack and walk to the nearest tube station.

The weather forecast is good. In Nottingham I meet neither friends nor family, and so avoid the delaying teapot or the jar of beer. Newer suburbs beyond the city centre cover the countryside I first explored, the horizon a line of domestic crenellations. Somebody on the bus tells me that shoddy blocks of flats under Balloon House Hill have been pulled down because plaster walls crumbled, doors didn't fit, and floors became mysteriously waterlogged. The bewildered tenants were moved out.

My bus stop is at Balloon House Hill, the traditional western outpost of the city. In the early nineteenth century it was the site of a Montgolfier-type ascent, and a balloonist in those days would have witnessed the smoke of industrial power from coalmines, mills and foundries, whereas now he would only see stillness and desolation.

Three ochre-coloured boxcars behind a hedge are used for storing hay, and I wonder if they were swilled up from the valley on a night of gales and floods, until I notice tracks to a coalpit marked on an old Ordnance Survey map.

My rucksack contains little more than a change of clothes and some food. The whistle and shunt of a far-off train makes me hungry, so I stop by a stile and shave nutritious slices from a Polish sausage, and cut some bread with my old airforce clasp knife. I pause at the panic wing-rattle of a wood pigeon rising from the dark button of a spinney, then go on eating.

Rufford

A privet hedgerow borders the path across Trowel Moor. Nettles, dog roses and deadly nightshade thicken the base. Flowers appear without fuss or notice, and go in the same manner. Sunlight through clouds that litter the sky spreads a netherlandish glow over rounded fields. Once ripped about for opencast coal, they look settled except where the motorway crosses, and even that is more vocal than visible.

A damp breeze shivers gobs of cuckoo spit on fresh arum lilies. Over a wall near the middle of Strelley seven bullocks and a horse share the umbrella of a chestnut tree. The 'most important church on the W outskirts of Nottingham', according to Elizabeth Williamson's guide book in the Pevsner Series, calls for scrutiny, but it comes too early in the walk, and neither my legs nor my inclination will allow me to go inside. Wormy sandstone of the walls is enlaced in thick wrists of ivy, and other buildings are on their way to being smothered.

In the days of my previous existence I bumped along this path in mud or dust by bicycle. The hedges are puny, not as I knew them on a summer's dusk, walking with a girlfriend and hoping to become invisible among the crushed harebells or succulent celandines. A wood has been erased for a motorway service station and, long after I cross, the noise is like a tide that never quite comes in, nor goes very far out.

A plaque on the church wall at Cossall says: 'Waterloo Memorial. Erected in 1877 in memory of three men who fought at the Battle of Waterloo'. John Shaw and Richard Waplington died at the battle, and Thomas Wheatley came back. Shaw, who was tall and, some say, mad drunk, killed eight Frenchmen before he fell exhausted and died.

Church Cottage was the home of Louise Burrows, one of D. H. Lawrence's early infatuations, and he made it into the setting of Honeymoon Cottage in his third and best novel, *The Rainbow*.

Down the hill lies the hamlet of Cossall Marsh, and the first odour from domestic fires brings positive nostalgia, though the feeling of emptiness makes it hard to believe I ever belonged to this intensely man-made part of the world.

Ilkeston Church is silhouetted across the River Erewash, much as Tom Brangwen saw it at the opening of *The Rainbow*: 'Two miles away, a church-tower stood on a hill, the houses of the little country town climbing assiduously up to it. Whenever one of the Brangwens in the fields lifted his head from his work, he saw the church tower at Ilkeston in the empty sky. So that as he turned again to the horizontal land, he was aware of something standing above him and beyond him in the distance.' These lines electrified me when I read them, because from then on I knew that one might write with advantage about the place one grew up in, and about the people who lived there.

Footpaths lead through the derelict area of the Erewash valley, one of many industrial revolution graveyards that litter Britain. The sides of a disused canal approach each other, and if left long enough alone will meet at lush reeds and brandy flagon waterlilies in the middle. The relatively sylvan way becomes a place of dead dogs, rotting car bodies and decomposing sofas.

In *The Rainbow* the canal was in its prime. Tom Brangwen came home one stormy night after a drinking bout in Nottingham, and his horse drew him half asleep along the muddy lane through Bilborough and Strelley. When he got home the canal burst its banks and he was drowned in the flood swirling around his farm, an event which again left Anna Lensky a widow.

A once white handsome farmhouse lies in ruins down the bank, slates shed from its roof, and a water butt squashed flat like a melon, as if a strongman has hit it with a drainpipe pulled off the wall. The front door has been kicked in, and holes take the place of windows.

In spite of the dereliction there is a persisting sound of far-off machinery, definite signs of life reasserting itself over the ruins; subtle, yet so positive that I stand a few moments in appreciation of the fact that an inborn talent for striving and inventiveness is a wonderful guarantee that life goes on.

Two men on the towpath are trying to drag some object out of the water with a length of cable, and the mud which drips from it gives off a sulphurous reek. Whatever they are after is caught in sludge and reeds, and not easy to dislodge. They are in a bit of a sweat, in fact. One says that they should go to the far side and pull from there. His mate doesn't think it worth walking a hundred yards to cross by the bridge, though he proves his goodwill in the venture by removing a festoon of weeds and bulrushes from a self-made grappling hook.

They grin as I pass, and answer my greeting as if caught in some illegal act. Their shaggy brown collie comes out of the water and walks towards me, head down, sly in one eye, and slowing pace as if bracing itself for the pleasurable effort of shaking the foul water from its back (and tail) when it is closest to me, so that everyone in the area will know where I have been. Perhaps the stare I put on saves me, not to mention my well-shod walking boots, for it doesn't ripple itself dry until well beyond range.

A path of soot, cinders and gravel leads to a car-breakers' yard. A gang of men at work on a mangled lorry eye me as if I am a policeman come to check licence plates. Few people walk in such areas on a weekday. There's nothing to come for, and no one lives close any more. Those who scavenge off such dumps guard the treasures of an empire, and seem to be always on the lookout for the reconnoitring skirmishers of a marauding army which would not only rob them blind of their hard-gained hoard, but kill them into the bargain.

They resume a clattering with iron bars as soon as I reach the canal, which from here has been filled in so effectively that it can no longer be called a landmark. A disused railway viaduct in a ruinous condition crosses the wide valley, which at one time meant two canals, a river, a mainline railway and several lanes.

Where the old canal goes under the eastern extension of the viaduct someone has painted BILL & AVRIL on the façade and, on the lesser brick supports, DAVE & AMANDA. Perhaps it is a test of modern love to climb with brush and paint pot, risking neck and spine, to inscribe the name of the beloved for everyone to see, a kind of *samizdat* of emotional loyalty when Bill would bring Avril (or Dave would lure Amanda) by a meandering yet cunningly planned route so that she would witness her name as if in lights. Or she would hate to be thus blazoned in print, and break off the connection for ever. There's no pleasing some people, Dave would then think.

Around this elegant ruin of a viaduct are lush meadows and ripe hedges. Vegetation proliferates. Dogs bark and cows low among a tenacious mixture of surrounding life. Footpaths that are heavily marked on the map are faint or non-existent on the ground. Farms and cottages have vanished, canals gone, and a new major road appears along the course of an old railway.

The most practical item of my hiker's gear is a combined telescope and prismatic compass, and though there are no prominent points on which to take bearings, I head for the hills and the noise of traffic, reaching a lane that takes me into a new suburb of Eastwood.

Night-stops, I decide, will be in bed-and-breakfast places, and I have a list from several sources in my notebook. In the older part of the town at half past four, I cross the main road to the Sun Inn and walk into the darkened hall. There is an intense smell of frying. I ring the bell but get no answer, and a guest on his way downstairs tells me that no one will show their faces until the pub part of the house opens at half past five.

I sit at a convenient table to write postcards bought from a shop on the main street, a set of mediocre drawings of buildings in the district associated with the early life of D. H. Lawrence.

There are directions on the hotel notice board as to how his birthplace and the various houses he lived in are to be found, as well as those described in his novels and stories. The postcard drawings do little justice to the importance of a town which attracts so many enquirers and pilgrims. Eastwood existed before Lawrence was born, and was said not to have cared much for his morals, but he seems to be the only reason many people come here from all over the world. He would find it ironic that the 'Lawrence Industry' is replacing that of the coalmines which once surrounded the place.

The noticeboard in the inn also displays names of people already lodging there, which suggests that a film unit is in the district, no rare thing these days, with Lawrence's centenary approaching.

The young landlord emerges from his apartments to tell me that

46

The Duke's Archway

no room is available for casual travellers, a fact not altogether regretted by one of them, since the place stands on a busy crossroads and I don't fancy being kept awake half the night by passing traffic.

From a telephone box outside I ring the Boat Inn, to be informed that their last rooms have gone. The final place on my list is the Two Counties Motel, and a brisk woman tells me that there is a room, though to reach it means going downhill and a mile out of town beyond New Eastwood which I passed coming in.

The further I go the less I like the idea of the motel, and walking by a busy two-way bypass suggests it might be a modern glass-and-plastic yurt-style establishment set by a beautifully landscaped flyover with matching traffic at room level. If so, there's always the ten-mile bus ride to Nottingham, and a bed there for the night.

But the signpost guides me onto a lane and by a farm. A young man on a horse is talking to a girl, and because the animal has its back to me I am ready to diverge into the safety of the lane, having been told by my blacksmith grandfather that you *never* walk behind a horse. But the man obligingly turns the animal so that I will not have to take evasive action.

The hotel is on the banks of the Erewash, a stream of soft water as if flowing between fur-lined banks. Beyond spreads a field in which horses graze. It's a view I half remember having seen as a child, and when I saw it then it was as if I had looked at it in some previous life. Anyone coming on it for the first time would surely accept the placid feeding of horses on rich grass by a stream of forceful water as something never to be forgotten. It has a primitive quality that helps to soothe and civilise.

A group of buildings, marked on an old map as a mill, is set apart from the noisy world and is now turned into a hotel. A television set snaps and howls in the dining-room, though I later sit before it, being too tired to do anything else. I am given a bill of eight pounds for bed, breakfast and evening meal while still involved with my pint of beer and substantial supper. The woman apologises for this premature collection of my reckoning on the grounds that I will be free to leave as early as I like in the morning.

Beyond the canal lies Shipley Boat Inn, and I am glad it wasn't able to accommodate me. Over the bar chip butties are advertised at forty pence apiece. I down a cup of coffee so quickly that the barmaid calls: 'Was it cold, duck?' I have to assure her that it wasn't, not caring to boast that I can put down a cup of scalding liquid quicker than anybody else. They might be fighting words in Eastwood.

The building is an enormous mansion, put up in the last century, perhaps for a self-made ironmaster of the time who wanted a house separated from the ordinary people he had grown up with. From a distance it looks huge and grey and ghostly, and now it is an inn at which there is no room, as well as a pub, and a mecca-like honky-tonk establishment that the gilded youth home in on with girlfriends, or husbands come with their wives in speedy little cars for a good night's drinking and a discotheque twopenny hop – Chatterley's Disco, they call it.

A footbridge over the railway gives a view of the canal going towards Eastwood, a way that in the morning will save me a walk by the eye-flashing bypass. A tongue of water rushes over the lock gate, on whose wings are painted: 'H. M. Rules' and 'Third Sex: Iron Maiden'. Cows opposite the towpath form an orderly queue to eat the rushes, a change of food from the ubiquitous pasture. Their hooves are sucked in by the mud, and because only one cow at a time can reach the succulent rushes, the others line up patiently and salivate. When the cow in front finishes the delicious mulch another takes its place.

The atmosphere is clearer because evening is close, one of those transitions from day to night at this latitude and in this season which seem to go on for ever. Two hundred yards west of the canal the brick buttresses of an uprooted railway span the minuscule Erewash, over which the canal and its towpath were carried by an unobtrusive aqueduct. Ruins sprout vegetation as in a Piranesi drawing, suggesting that a modern draughtsman could wander on a working holiday around the Erewash area before, unlike the grander ruins of Rome, such industrial archeology disappears. There are already signs that it is being cleaned up. When the area was in full productive blast

Newstead Colliery

no doubt it seemed hellish (though not as loathsome as some people think), but now that the mighty Lucifer has fallen there does seem a different kind of poetry in it.

The ruins of ancient Rome were the constructions of emperors and popes, while these crumbling brick-built kilns and culverts, bridges and foundries were made for trade, and though they didn't give happiness – they weren't meant to, and in any case what could? – they provided employment and a certain social stability which is now on the way out. It was fashionable, among those who never had to work, to wish that these industrial areas would recede from their offended eyesight, and now that normal evolution is doing it a vacuum is perceived in human endeavour that will not so easily be filled. People can't make Indian blankets and play ring-around-the-Greenwood-Tree. If prophets are not honoured it is because they are often so wrong and misguided. D. H. Lawrence loathed such manifestations of industrialism, but then, loathing is so subjective – though only a bit more so than love. The insane ranting in Mellors's letter at the end of *Lady Chatterley's Lover* was the screed of a sick man.

Crossing another derelict canal brings me to a bridge over the bypass which, in the morning, will make a more bucolic route to the southern fringes of Eastwood. The isolated spot is strewn with heaps of household rubbish. Set apart from the main tipping ground is a brown-lacquered tin trunk. I undo the latch and lift the curving lid, to see only a half brick inside. A piece of folded cardboard smells of smokey dampness and, when straightened, reveals the exhortation O GOD OF ISRAEL BLESS THIS HOUSE – framed words once hung on a parlour wall and beamed at a household which perhaps benefited from the message. The family has come and gone, the house demolished. When the grandmother died, or was taken blind and senile to die in the hospital, her family no longer felt there was a God whose help would do them much good.

From the bridge of the filled-in canal an old man in a cap looks at where horse-drawn barges once plied, where he had scouted for minnows, and walked with the girl he had courted. He wishes me good evening, in a voice as if the thoughts I had taken him from were not easily forgotten.

It is almost dark. The same young man canters by on his horse. The stone archway leading into the car park of the hotel has a notice saying that it spans the Nottinghamshire and Derbyshire border – hence the name of the place. At ten-thirty, tired from a twenty-kilometre walk, I read a few pages of Adrian's *Life of Alexander the Great*. The noise of a train disturbs the valley. From somewhere comes the long-drawn-out whinnying of a horse, a sound which only increases the feeling of peace, and impels me to put out the light.

Feet, plugged into earth, are pulled free. Fingertips are drawn back from oblivion. I wake at seven-twenty without being called, and ten minutes later a pot of tea is brought in. The night had severed connection with normal life, and from now on I live from minute to minute, only belonging to where my feet are put down. I'll have nothing to think about except which direction to walk in, or whether or not it will rain. Such elementary problems are a vacation for the soul. The rucksack is easy to pack, because only necessities litter the bed.

Cows in the field look as though they haven't moved all night, but someone has been out early and put a match to the rubbish tip, and acrid smoke redolent of such dumps everywhere reaches me a hundred yards before I come to the place, reminding me of when, as a child, I would pass the day over smouldering acres in the hope of finding something of value. But older and more experienced denizens of the rubbish heaps, struggling to earn the odd shilling to augment their dole, scrambled over the tipped-out loads before they were set on fire, or rain washed them away, or pestilence put them out of bounds, threatening me if I came too close. Occasionally, early in the morning, or late in the afternoon after everyone else had gone, a lorry from a sweet factory brought in a mass of bull's-eyes or caramels clammed together with bits of paper and sawdust that could be cleaned under a cold tap; or a few cracked cups from Players' canteen; or wood from a building site that could be taken home for the fire; or metal from the Raleigh to be raked out and sold for a few pence to a scrap dealer – big events on that dumping ground which these Eastwood fumes took me vividly back to, so that I looked through the present tip with the professional eye of someone who has not practised for a long time.

Little can be forgotten as long as the sense of smell remains. Here there is paper, wet cartons, old clothes, scraps of plastic toy – nothing that even in the old days would have been much to get excited about. The terraces of rammel that I roamed as an urchin have long since been covered by factories and warehouses.

Such recollections put me into a good mood. In any case, the day is new enough for birdsong to be dominant in the noise-world. It isn't raining, nor is the sun shining, but several horses that pasture tranquilly gather beneath a tree as if a shower might be on the way.

Eastwood straddles a ridge, and by nine o'clock I am walking along the main street to send off my dozen cards from the post office. An old man by the counter shows interest when I enquire the price of stamps to Israel. He knew someone who went to that place for a year, he says, a gentile though, who sang like an angel and got work on an orange farm. The only book he took was his Bible. I tell him I've been there several times.

'If I was a bit younger,' he laughs, 'I'd be off like a shot.'

Streets down the northern slope of the hill have been reconditioned, but the old style kept. I haven't been to Eastwood since December 1950, when I came on a trolley bus from Nottingham. Interested in everything about D. H. Lawrence, I had written to Alderman Willie Hopkins, who then invited myself and Ruth Fainlight to tea. He was about ninety years old, and had been an older friend to 'Bert' when he was alive. I forget what we talked about, but he gave us a good tea, and since we were all knowledgeable I'm sure the meeting was lively.

The Lawrence Cult had hardly begun, but today a museum has been made out of his birthplace and a couple of Americans and an English schoolteacher wait at the door for opening time at half past nine. After paying our twenty pence we file into the shop-windowed parlour, which has been reinstated to that of a miner's dwelling of 1885. Lawrence lived here till he was two.

Enid Goodband, the middle-aged local woman who is the curator of the museum, has devoted much time to accumulating objects of the period, in which she was helped by well-wishers of the area. My grandparents' cottage of the 1930s, which hadn't altered since they were married in 1890, marks the furnishing as realistic, even nostalgic.

Mrs Goodband considers that Lawrence should be honoured by the people among whom he was born, and about whom he has written with the profound understanding of a great writer. The area has been stamped so much on world consciousness that those who read his novels in faraway places feel a need to come and see the town and country round about.

The parlour which one enters off the street was the pride of the house, used only on Sunday and for special occasions. Those who lived there never entered by it, but went in by a door from the backyard. Likewise in my grandparents' house, I never once saw the front door opened all the years I went there.

In the Lawrence parlour there are chairs, a sofa, and a round table with its huge Bible in the middle, on which is placed an aspidistra, a green spreading crown of life on the Book of Law and Wisdom. Mrs Goodband knows Lawrence's works and his life story as if it were her own, as well as what people have written about him. Such extensive knowledge merits an honorary degree in D. H. Lawrence, and I hope some university either in this country or in the United States will one day do her the honour.

The second room of the ground floor is the kitchen, also of the period. The black-leaded fireplace has a built-in boiler on the left for heating the bath water. There were many panics in our house when, after a coal fire had been burning a whole winter's day, someone used the water but forgot to refill the small square boiler, which was then replenished in a hurry for fear it would burst or crack.

I hadn't seen one for forty years, a little black box of water with its iron lid, and tongue of a handle that you had to hold with a sock

Clumber Park

so that it would not burn the fingers. You ladled out the scalding liquid into a bath already a third filled with cold. There was never enough, and an extra pan was boiling on the fire, with another on the hob keeping hot, so that the four of us got a hot dip on Saturday night that for the rest of the week was remembered as a bath.

Other items of the miner's life are a lamp, and a snap tin in which he carried his food to the pit – like a set of army mess tins except that they 'snapped' shut to keep out the coal dust. It was a good house and, as our guide reminded us, Mrs Lawrence 'kept it like a new pin'.

The front upstairs room is the master bedroom, with the sort of bed in which Lawrence might have been born. There is another room on the same floor, and more space in an attic, not exactly ample, but adequate for a family of four or five, as the Lawrences then were. Nor was the house a slum, according to the standards of my own early experience. In 1885 the street had been up for about forty years, like a house today built in the 1930s, some of which seem almost new, and certainly more habitable than the cardboard flats which become derelict in ten years.

The backyard has its wash house. Under the copper boiler a fire was lit to get hot water for the weekly wash. An ancient mangle squeezed so much water out of the clothes that there was little need for ironing. A wooden 'dolly ponch' bashed the dirt out of the clothes on Monday morning. Perhaps things weren't so automatic and ergonomic in those days, but most homes had things organised to as neat a pitch as was possible.

Back in the parlour a gas mantle burns whitish yellow from the ceiling, and Mrs Goodband is concerned because a brown speck means she will have to put in another soon, and they aren't easy to come by these days. It's gone ten o'clock, and I want to set out over the hills to Newstead, so I sign the visitors' book and make a move for the door.

She spots my name, and we talk about Lawrence and his works for half an hour. She seems to live and breathe in order to keep the memory of him fresh for Eastwood and its environs, which has been no easy matter, either for her or other sympathisers. Many people couldn't forgive him both for the life he led and for the kind of books he was supposed to have written, which I imagine few of his local critics have read. It is easier to talk of him at the present, though a core of resistance remains, especially among the old, and the so-called neighbourhood elect.

A double row of houses down the hill known as 'The Breach', where Lawrence spent most of his young life, are more substantial than those of the street on which he was born. I set off along the lane towards Coney Green Farm, and then on to Willey Wood Farm about a mile away, a gentle climb of two hundred feet. When I turn to look, Eastwood sprawls up the opposite hill, but in front there is green countryside, flesh that is sweetest when close to the bone, bucolic pockets described in precise and loving detail by Lawrence.

Going down the hill to Moorgreen Reservoir, the thousand yards by a main road is far enough in traffic to make me glad when I get to the bottom and turn again on to a footpath. In *Women in Love* the Criches at the nearby house give a party, and the lake is called Willey Water which was 'blue and fair, the meadows sloped down in sunshine on one side, the thick dark woods dropped steeply on the other'. During the festivities the daughter of the house, Diana, is drowned and when the water is drained she's found with 'her arms tight round the neck of the young man, choking him' – Dr Brindell who had tried to rescue her.

The woods look somewhat scruffy, the water metallic and half dead, and I only want to get into High Park Wood that packs the darkened east side. Silence is a luxury, to be sought for and, if necessary, endured like a refugee. The spirit bruises itself against noise. The multiple dinning machines of modern life box in any thought, however trivial. There is no way beyond the surrounding perimeter of engines. They roar overhead, blotting out the sky.

But not in this damp wood, not yet, only the crunch of a few dead twigs blown by the wind. The feet alone can get you to silence. Lodge gates channel me into damper air, and to a part of Nottinghamshire, on the eastern side of the Erewash Valley, that has its own special

Lawrence's Birthplace

character. The emphasis of Lawrence has made it slightly unreal, and I find it necessary to put his works out of mind for a while, which is not more difficult than forgetting Hardy's novels while in Dorset.

I see the land freshly because it is finally more powerful than those who write about it. The land is there for people to walk over, and for writers to use like farmers, to harvest it into their books for the benefit of consuming readers, who reap its food for the soul as surely as a farmer produces earthly bread. But you don't know the land until you feel the texture under your boots, view the shades of green, notice the dullness, smell the bark and loam. Only then does it come to life.

Each generation of writers describes the countryside afresh so as to keep the appreciation of it alive. The people are related to the landscape, and change little, in spite of technology and the meretricious overlay of flash advertising. A writer relates people to their landscape, which thereby deepens the portrait of both. When this relationship vanishes from writing, art loses its centre.

Notice boards proclaim the privacy of woods beyond the wire fencing. I dodge mud and waterholes along the lane. A mile north, at the ruins of Felley Mill, and when I ascend along the edge of a wood, a strong hay-like odour comes from grass and flowers. Few fields are cultivated, most given over to pasture, and the woods and their hedges left untouched, like despatch boxes not to be opened for fifty years.

Twenty horses were grazing in the Eastwood area. Why did I count them? They were placid and uncaring, and after admiring the beauty of even the meanest, left me little else to do. The sharpness of the eye increases, the impact on the senses goes deep, but I counted, all the same. I can't see and not count. The senses form a harmony of response when out on foot. Pedestrian speed becomes an amble, a conscious slowing down of the self. But one can go too fast, and see less than one should, even in walking. After a while the head goes down, and you look at where to put the feet, and the lungs strain until their physical connection to the eyes causes them to tire as well, dimming even the vision and the will to see.

The eye gazes idly at ferns, fronds, grasses and flowers, but also maintains an unmistakable view along the path going eastward. A line of wood stretches to the south, ups and downs at between four and five hundred feet. Far underfoot the geology changes, marked on the map by a layer-cake of complications: the ossified wood of coal measures, then over Lower Mottled Sandstone and Middle Parmian Marl, through Boulder Clay to Permian Marl and Magnesian Limestone around Hucknall and Lynby. Geology determines the earth's clothing, and regulates the number of people who can exist on it. Sandstone country on the western side of the county supports those people who work in the coal mines – at the moment. The eastern part of the county is clay, and the agricultural population is less numerous.

Grey clouds are of a sort that aren't ready to make rain. The path becomes a distinct 'ride' into the wood and goes south. The M1 is close, though the road is not visible, and because of the baffling effect of the trees I have no certainty as to its direction. According to the map the path should veer left and reach a footbridge over the M1, but suddenly there are many paths, used perhaps by dumper trucks for the construction of the motorway. If I go southerly for too long I might tumble down Robin Hood's Well, which is marked as in that part of the forest.

So I double back and find the cat-plank from which to view motors and lorries streaming north and south, each vehicle steered by the encapsulated absorption of its driver. When I'm in one of them, my car on auto-pilot, I see little more than the unrolling road, ever on the alert for a blowout, a jack-knifed lorry, or an insane overtaker on the opposite lane catapulting along a malign trajectory towards me. From my present crow's-nest I see them madcapping to their destinations, and feel lucky that I am out on my own two feet.

Annesley Lodge, demolished to make way for the long sinuous sabre-cut of the road, was indicated on Robert Thornton's plan of Annesley Park in 1790. Annesley Hall was the home of Mary Chaworth, one of Byron's earliest loves, which gave him a singular view of the area, though in the summer there is something uplifting about it, not entirely deadened by the motorway:

Hills of Annesley, bleak and barren,
Where my thoughtless childhood strayed,
How the northern tempests, warring,
Howl about thy tufted shade!

Misk Hill intervenes between me and Hucknall, which I often cycled to and walked over after a day's work in the factory, for the fresh air and a fine view. The air wasn't always as clean as it might have been, and the view was occasionally obscured by rain or mist.

For old times' sake I ascend by the farm and through the wood, on to an open plateau of green stubble, 526 feet above sea level, to look across at the zone of pine trees which I just walked through. The open land between is a purple slope of bare field. To the south-east the sprawl of Nottingham darkens under grey cloud, and coagulates at its centre, seven miles away. Misk Hill hasn't yet been captured: houses are kept at bay. Cows graze in the next field, and it is a green and peaceful place from which a young man can look down on Nottingham and decide whether to stay a lifetime with his own tribe in familiar streets, or set off into uncertain geographies beyond – a kind of Rastignac's Perch of the Midlands.

I wrote a poem on that common theme:

VIEW FROM MISK HILL

Armies have already met and gone.
When the best has happened
The worst is on its way
Beware of its return in summer
When fields are grey and should be green
Rubbing scars with ash and sulphur.

Full moon clears the land for its own view,
With fangs it would bereave this field
of hayrick and sheep.

In the quiet evening birds fly
Where armies are not fighting yet.
He looks a long way on from now,
At where he'll walk
A cratered highway with all hedges gone.

Green land dips and smells of fire
Of life. Topography is wide down there
The moon waxes then emaciates
Birds fatten before migration
On fields enriched for harvest.

Smoke of summer hangs between earth and sky,
On ground where armies have not fought
But will as he passes through.

The scenery changes, as if the motorway divides two distinct
topographical areas. As well as farms, coppices and plantations there
is a sort of cement works which gives the fields a bare and dusty look.
Huge lorries harden the lane, and I step into the hedge to let one by.
In Briar Plantation most of the trees have been cut down, and sitting
on a dead log I eat another lunch of rye bread and garlic sausage.

The threat to the countryside near towns has almost gone, because
the population has stopped growing, and is even falling. Third World
Marxists and members of the Festival of Light may deplore the fact,
but it seems good that the rural peace of Misk Hill is now beyond
the high water mark of the bungalow tide.

Only dogs seem lively while going through a farmyard. I walk the
obligatory mile between the outskirts and Hucknall market-place.
The reason for going there (apart from the fact that there's no way
round by footpath) is to visit the church where Byron is buried, or
at least those of his organs which had the good luck to get back from
Missolonghi in 1824. There is some dispute as to exactly what parts
of him do lie beneath the slab of rosso antico, but his heart is
certainly at rest on that spot.

An immense procession followed the hearse from Nottingham on

First Novel Café

Friday 16 July 1824, to see his remains interred with the other eight generations of Byrons. The poet was honoured by the populace because in his maiden speech in the House of Lords at the age of twenty-four he spoke on behalf of the starving weavers of Nottingham, in a debate on the Frame Breaking Bill which stipulated that the penalty for frame-breaking was to be death.

'I have been in some of the most oppressed provinces of Turkey,' Byron said, 'but never under the most despotic of infidel governments did I behold such squalid wretchedness as I have seen since my return in the very heart of a Christian country.' He went on: 'How can you carry the Bill into effect? Can you commit a whole country to their own prisons? Will you erect a gibbet in every field, and hang up men like scarecrows?'

So they did not forget to mourn him when his body was brought home from Greece where, as the plain mural tablet on the south wall of the chancel says: 'He engaged in the glorious attempt to restore to the country her ancient freedom and renown.' The family vault was so full that his remains are only three feet below the level of the floor, a spot marked with a wreath of inlaid brass, on which is written: 'Byron, born Jan. 22 1788; died Apl. 19, 1824'.

After appropriate salutations I cross the market-place, and go through streets of small houses out of town. Beyond the coal mine of Lynby lies the village, and the attractive public house called the Duke of Newcastle seems to beckon me with a pint of shandy like the frothing jug of sherbet in paradise. A snack of pastry and cup of coffee in Hucknall left an intense thirst, but three o'clock struck a few seconds ago, and all doors of the pot house are closed as firmly as if fifty gunners of the South Nottinghamshire Hussars Yeomanry are expected to come through on their way to annual camp.

A lane out of the village, after a kilometre, becomes a footpath leading directly to Newstead Abbey. It is not a right of way, but will save time, and I trust to good luck and navigation to get me through.

A large straggle-haired black dog barks out of a cottage garden as if to tear me to pieces, but a few gruff phrases in a Nottingham voice leave no doubt that I will put my boot to its ribs should it come too

64

close. A woman stares at me but says nothing, and I go on my way as if I walk that route every day.

Several boards announce – as if one is not enough – that the property before me is a quarry (a private quarry, what's more), a personal private confidential quarry – or words to that effect – which should by no means be entered into. Further notice boards at fairly regular intervals stress that the road into the area is closed, state plainly that everyone should keep out, and imply – one of the boards actually says so (I've been waiting for it) – that trespassers will certainly be prosecuted. In view of such exhortations to temptation, to continue on my otherwise peaceful way is irresistible. I am not a conspicuous figure in my shades of olive-green, meaning that should I stop walking and sit by a hedge no one will see me from more than a hundred yards. Camouflage is a great invention!

I get over a five-barred gate without smashing it, or even tearing my clothes. After more woodland, the reddish acreage of a quarry opens out. My map is only half the scale of the one used yesterday, and lacks detail for easy tactical navigation, so I put it in my pocket and walk to the hut, intending to ask the way to Newstead if I am challenged. It's locked, and no one is about. Perhaps it's full of dynamite. But the area seems to have been abandoned long ago, though why are the notices so new – and so insistent? A boy's adventure story swings into gear, but I forbear giving the plot.

A series of limestone quarries, and marked as such, are shown on early Ordnance Survey maps. It's amazing, I found later, armed with a magnifying glass, how many more names, and how much more information per square inch, is engraved on them than is printed on modern versions.

Mr Laird's book on Nottinghamshire of 1820 says: 'very extensive quarries, of a reddish sandstone, in immense quantities, are now worked in full near Mansfield . . .' and I believe this is where it came from. There is no fixed path, and a track beyond the quarry is barely evident. Continuing north, I try not to tread on the corn. My presence must be obvious for miles to an acute observer because the stealth of a jungle advance, and care in the art of concealment, mean

Neighbours – Eastwood

nothing when a covey of partridges and a pack of pigeons with all-round vision lift with a clatter of wings and make off towards the clouds.

I move with speed, though I can't easily be seen. The noise of disturbed birds need not indicate a trespasser. They probably panic four times a day, like clockwork, so unless brought face to face with a gamekeeper I won't be intercepted till I am back on a public lane, when it will no longer be an issue.

Nevertheless, out in the open I feel conspicuous and uncomfortable. Climbing a combination of hedge-fence-and-wall into a wood, I wade through ferns, high nettles and brambles, to the lowest part where there is a stream, and steer north in semi-darkness of overgrown foliage, a more feasible route until it becomes swampy.

Bushes and bracken hinder movement, but an advance is possible, indeed necessary. If I were on the run, and able to get here unnoticed, with a rucksack of supplies, and a .22 air pistol for potting rabbits, I could lie up for days, even weeks, and would be safer than in the more extensive purlieus of the Dukeries or Sherwood Forest proper.

The art of concealment is born with me. I move with ease through territory belonging to someone else, but the personality of whoever owns the land is subordinated to mine while I am in it, though I have no idea of what his or her personality consists. As a novelist I can make it up, and gamble on the fact that I am right, because all puzzles eventually fit if put together with patience and imagination.

The fact is that someone is the owner, and I am a marauder on his or her land. In childhood trespassing was a way of life and, after growing up (as far as one can grow up) with what alacrity one goes back to it! Or thinks one does, until sunlight comes through the trees and a fence indicates a bridlepath.

To get out of the wood is liberation indeed, a sudden change from being in darkness to a track that leads back to the light. The dark wood is for self-preservation but, sooner or later, when ambition for the illumination beckons, you realise it has never been enough, except as a short cut.

At Quarry Banks Farm my way is plain, because after another mile of leafy and undulating lane I come out of a deep cutting to see the grand façade of Newstead Abbey.

My thirst is so ferocious that the tearoom is my first objective. In any case, I learn that fifteen minutes must elapse before the next conducted tour of Byron's apartments. A couple of plastic cups of teabag tea is as welcome as a saline spring to a man just out of the Persian desert, for the liquid is metallic and unnecessarily foul, the sort of low brew which, when sweetened, makes me wonder whether I've put salt in instead of sugar. Having walked the day on barely a pint of liquid there is much to make up for.

In the tea place part of the Abbey a dozen ageing men and women, in varying stages of senility, are on an outing from their home. They sit at tables, and are in the charge of a girl who looks no more than thirteen. She goes from one group to another enquiring whether or not they need anything. The blank faces furthest gone re-create a mask-like smile.

The most eroded senses feel her nearness: 'Have you got enough tea, duck? Was it nice? Did you enjoy it, then? I'm sure you did. It *was* nice, worn't it? Would you like some more of that lovely cake? Have a bit more cake. Go on. It wain't kill you. You've lost your handbag? We'll soon find it. Look, it's down there on the floor.'

She sets it by the old lady's teacup. A woman to whom it doesn't belong pulls it open, and gets her wrist slapped. A man can't find his pipe, and must have it back, where he can see it, or feel the familiar hump in his pocket, otherwise life has no meaning. There is only his beloved pipe between him and the void. He is too far out of his own airspace to love anything else. His soul is limitless tundra without it.

Feel in the *other* pocket, she says. He does. No good. She finds it in the lining of his mackintosh. His friend strikes a match with shivering hands, and they light pipes together as if just back from a stint in the trenches. They'll be getting on the bus soon, so do any of them want to go to the toilet? She leads two to the door, and one of the more capable people goes with them.

She is like a mother of forty, in her concern, humour and energy, a good little busybody of a shepherdess. Perhaps she's older than I think, but she certainly knows how to make her charges feel cared for, and how to look after them.

Newstead Abbey changed owners several times in the nineteenth century, but Sir Julian Cahn presented it to the city of Nottingham in 1931. He also gave a cricket ground to the city, at one time fielding his own team, whose matches were watched by thousands.

Paying the same amount as to see Lawrence's house at Eastwood, I'm shown the place which Byron swore he would never sell, though he was forced to when creditors clamoured for their money. He was paid a hundred thousand pounds, the equivalent of four or five million today. Leaving England, he never came back, unless he could be said to have returned on the hearse which brought his bits and pieces back to Hucknall Church.

He doesn't get a good character reference from our guide, who mentions with disdain how he used the chapel to house his menagerie, and employed the monks' mortuary as a plunge bath for himself and his dog Boatswain. Byron inherited Newstead when he was eleven, but his spirit as a free man and a poet denied him the art of good management. You can't have everything. His extravagance and generosity, or profligacy if you like, was not tolerated by the moral climate of England. Some comparison might be made with his neighbour Lawrence, who also felt he was hounded out of the country.

Our group is led around the cloisters which, we are informed, resemble those of Westminster Abbey. Byron's bedroom is more or less as he left it, and contains various relics, as well as manuscripts, first editions and books about him.

An establishment within vast grounds, even the unruined part was too extensive to be borne by a young poet if he wasn't to subside into a talentless life under its weight. His subconscious told him to get out, and any method was valid, be it by debt or scandal, or both. England drove him away because it hated him, while he was happy to depart for good because he loved England but did not like it.

In the sultry air, small green flies get squashed between the pages of my notebook. I imagine I can hear the ghost of Boatswain growling from the ruins, but it's someone's mongrel by the waterfall. A single angler sits on the lake bank while I write postcards.

My objective is Mansfield, eleven kilometres away, so I set off along the winding lane of Swincotte Dale, then cross the main road to Ravenshead, an area of new houses settled by commuters from Nottingham. Cars are being washed, hosepipes are spraying gardens, and children are riding bicycles from school. Several hundred spick-and-span acres have neither club, pub, chapel nor, as far as I can see, shops of any kind. But I suppose those who live there appreciate the countryside rolling away on every flank.

After the first of three ridges before Mansfield I get into Fountain Dale, in which glen stands the cloven rock of the Druid's Stone, a fourteen-foot geological freak no doubt used by founder members of the Ivy League. It is also the scene of Robin Hood's encounter with that pot-bellied prelate Friar Tuck, a contest which lasted from ten in the morning till four in the afternoon, a fair day's work for an outlaw, if ever there was one.

Every copse, conery and clearing has some connection with Robin Hood and his Merry Gang, and as I am the only person for miles I don't fancy a chance meeting. A public right of way crosses the three ridges, part of the track going by the eastern side of Harlow Wood, map-marked as Thieves Wood, another reminder of Robin's whereabouts, or so you might think, but in 1817 it was the scene of the brutal murder of seventeen-year-old Elizabeth Shepherd who was on her way from Papplewick to Mansfield to look for work. Charles Rotherham raped her, then pulled a stake from the hedge and killed her. He was suspected of the crime when trying to sell her shoes and umbrella in the Three Crowns at Redhill. His previous record was that of twelve years as a soldier, having served through the Peninsular Campaign with Wellington's Army. But he died on the gibbet instead of the battlefield.

A paperboy on his round whistles along on his bike to Firs Farm. The sprawl of Mansfield comes in sight, but there are two miles of

70

wstead Abbey

built-up area before knowing whether I'll be able to get a bed there for the night. I am hungry, certainly thirsty, and sore at the right ankle, having covered the last seven kilometres in an hour and a half. I hope for a bed-and-breakfast sign at some house window which will stop me short of the middle of town, so that there will be no need to traipse all the way out again in the morning.

But I see nothing. At seven o'clock the market-place is deserted, though stalls are already erected for tomorrow's business. With banks and boozers mostly in side streets, the homely middle of the town must look much as it did a century ago. I ask the way to the Midland Hotel, the only name on my overnight stopping list, and the man who gives directions in a Polish accent is maybe one of those miners who helped to get the country back on its feet in the late forties, when labour in the pits was so short.

The Midland has no vacancy, though a girl at the desk tells me where I might find one. She shows me a short cut through the business part of the hotel into a saloon by whose bar I down a pint of shandy in a few seconds.

I lose my sense of direction in the market-place, but with the help of my compass I find north and set off along the Pleasley road to the Fernleaf Hotel. The only food served is breakfast, and as it's impossible to wait that long for something to eat I change into plimsolls for a walk back into town, feeling marvellously light without the rucksack.

A food bar is the only place offering what's needed. The day's zig-zagging totals thirty kilometres, which I calculate on the map with a fancy little rolling device while waiting for a plate of chips and meat and two pots of tea.

A forty-year-old woman wearing a fur beret sits a few tables away. She smokes one cigarette after another, and has a cup of tea which she doesn't touch. The waitresses know her, and are friendly with everyone. Even a trio of rowdy youths don't break their humour. The woman looks as if she treats the place as her refuge, from streets populated by demons she wishes to avoid. Perhaps she is waiting for someone. She may, equally, wonder what I am doing here, though we take care not to catch each other's eye. Her face is calm, sallow yet well fleshed, and she looks as if just far enough from some previous trouble of the soul to start feeling easy again, but barely so, unable to forget the worst aspects of her experience, whatever it was. If she is waiting for someone to turn up I'll never know who it is, because I pay my bill and leave.

Thighs and ankles ache, and both feet are sore, but a hot bath eases them. I hope all will be well in the morning as I read more of Alexander the Great's victories and tribulations. Sleep, when it comes, is shallow. My cell-like room on the ground floor is close to a main route from town which leads to the motorway. Such noise is like being on the end of a runway, the perimeter track lights on, and four-engined Second World War transport planes landing overhead before coming to a halt at the control tower. I tell myself now and again that a good night's rest is being had, which is like no sleep at all. When I drift into oblivion I am pulled back by an attack of cramp.

A mile south-west of Mansfield lies a reservoir, but a tale attaches to it from when it was dry land and known as King's Mill. It received the name after an incident in the reign of Henry II. The king was separated from his hunting cronies after dusk, and was lost. A miller found him and took him to his home. The king claimed to be only a poor courtier. The miller poured him a drink, and brought out a huge vension pasty for their supper. The king found it fine and dainty, and asked how it was that a miller could live so well.

'We eat like this every day,' the man laughed, hinting that there was plenty more where that came from. 'We don't pay for it, either.'

'And where *does* it come from?' asked the poor courtier.

'Any idiot ought to know that,' the miller told him. 'Real venison, it is. We just help ourselves to the King's deer from the forest. I'm never without two or three stowed in the attic.'

The courtier went to sleep, sharing straw with the miller's son.

Sherwood Forest

After next morning's breakfast, which consisted of more of the same thing, the King's party, who had been looking for him all night, found him outside the miller's house and prostrated themselves before him. On realising who his guest had been the miller expected that he and his family would be hanged on the spot for breaking the harsh forest laws. He grovelled, thinking he was about to be decapitated when the King took out his sword, but the King –

> His kind courtesy for to requite,
> Gave him great living and made him a knight.

A glance at the map – between finishing a dish of cornflakes and starting on eggs, sausage, bacon and fried bread – shows me that having come into town through two miles of streets from the south-east, there will be no avoiding a slog through a similar stretch of built-up unerogenous zone to the north-west in order to reach open country. Fortunately the massive breakfast will keep me sufficiently fuelled until lunch, certainly more so than after a continental plate of bread and butter. It used to be said that an Englishman would even get himself hanged for a good breakfast, though in my case twenty miles a day seems a better alternative.

In presenting my bill, and having seen my name in the registration book, the waiter asks if I am related to the late Sir Percy who, early in his career, was chief constable at nearby Chesterfield. I imply that my family could never have been connected to such a law-enforcing figure. He says he's heard the name in some other connection, but I am not able to enlighten him, being anxious to pick up my rucksack and be off, which is a pity, because in my hurry I forget to have the tea flask filled, a serious lack in view of the day's trek.

Market stalls are stocked for trading, so I buy fruit to augment my provisions. Since Hucknall I have been on the 1:50,000 scale of mapping. I like the metric system recently introduced by the Ordnance Survey (never having been a stick-in-the-mud inch-to-a-mile man myself) except for the confused numbering of contour lines, which is still in feet. There is no difficulty however in navigating out of town because all streets are marked, though not named. A six-inch scale would be necessary for that, and though they would prove interesting even on the country parts of my walk, I do not have a trolley on which to haul the numerous sheets necessary to cover the whole area.

The river Maun, of Mansfield, means a valley, which maunders mournfully, and to get away from it demands an uphill walk through streets of newish houses on to a ridge. Domestic coalsmoke on a summer's day is homely but stifling. On a further hump between the Maun and what is mapped as Vicar Water flows a stream even more of a nonentity, which serves as a drainage channel for Forest Town, and for Clipstone colliery, which was the first and last coal pit I went down, twenty years ago. I was to write the commentary for a film on how miners spend their leisure, something I would be able to do more effectively if I also saw how they worked. For days afterwards I was spitting dust, and drinking gallons of any liquid to slake my thirst. I made the mistake, after coming up, of imbibing in the Miners' Welfare what the bandmaster recommended – pints of Guinness reinforced with port-style wine, which I've never drunk since.

There is no more escaping coalmines in this area than of getting away from the haunts of Robin Hood. A dusty cinder track running along the side of Vicar Water is hard on the feet. The rear gardens of Forest Town's tenement-like buildings back on to it, the headstocks of a mine to the right. The smell announces Newlands Farm well beforehand, and nobody is in the yard as I go through. The country seems to have been abandoned in places, different I suppose to fifty years ago, when people had to use the short cuts of the footpath system.

But the dust kicked up, as I walk in the sun by Vicar Water, gives way to the pavements of the colliery village. A man in shirtsleeves working on his patch of garden wishes me good morning.

The geological map spells coal, a landscape which permits nothing in the way of agriculture except the long-term growing of forest on thinnish soil. A pretty map is a joy for ever, and the prettiest is streaked with green and blue and yellow, patched with purple and the grey of coal measures, as if a child has mixed a football of plasticine colours and cleaved the sphere in two to reproduce the design on paper.

I bring my eyes up from the map to see green dark forest on one side, colliery spoil heaps to the right, and the houses of Old Clipstone down a dip but coming up quickly at the rate I am walking. A pub in the village is prominently marked on my ever-encouraging ordinary landscape map, and at ten-thirty I hope it will be one of those with a card in the window advertising morning coffee. Not even that. It's bolted and barred, and there's neither shop nor store – nor even a filling station with a freezer of tinned shandy.

Under a triangle of railways the footpath climbs northerly towards the woods, and at the top of the ridge stands the isolated 'Duke's Archway'. The building – a quaint concoction to come across on a lonely walk – looks scholastic and ecclesiastical and is in fact a copy of the Priory Gateway at Worksop built by the Duke of Portland in 1842. In three niches on the south side are figures of Robin Hood, Little John and Maid Marian, while on the north face are effigies of Friar Tuck and Alan-a-Dale. The upper rooms were used as a school as recently as the First World War. The local people looked on it, and probably still do, as the Duke's Folly, but to me it marks an impressive entrance to Sherwood Forest.

A man tidying the gravel drive asks if I am lost, his tone implying that I have no business walking this way, and that it is unfair of me to have bought a map and discovered the red dots of a footpath thereon – an unwelcome stranger to cross his line of vision.

'It's a nice building you've got there.' What else can I say? The remark satisfies him that I'm not the advance guard of a mob on its way from Nottingham to burn it down. All the same, I get no friendly word as he turns to continue his clearing up.

Crossing the main road I climb over a gate on to an asphalted track that goes into the forest but is not a right of way. A profusion of plants and flowers grow to either side: agrimony, forget-me-nots, white campion, thistles, briars, buttercups, elderberry flowers, ferns, full oaks and dark fir trees – the rich flora of Sherwood disturbed only by the fellow-trespassing sound of the cuckoo.

The paved lane runs along the edge of the trees, then veers north into a denser part of the wood known as Robin Hood's Larder. A chaffinch balances on the topmost dead twig of a lightning-blasted oak, its legs so thin that they are invisible, so that its fat feathered body seems to rest on a cushion of air.

Straight tracks radiate like compass points, and I change course towards Centre Tree, a two-hundred-year-old landmark ripe for the knacker's lightning. A few mature arms are cracked at the elbow, and cast-off limbs lie scattered as if the tree has gone childish in old age and thrown branches aside to prove it has a will (though not a mind) of its own. Yet it is green in places, dark and gnarled, with a tenacious grip that will draw succour for more years than I have left, even if only to spite the supercilious beeches and encroaching birches.

A mile further on, Major Oak is the real old grand-daddy of them all, enormous though not high. Brooding and threatening, if it decided to move, the world would have to make way. It would breakfast on Worksop, dine on Doncaster, nosh on Nottingham and, in an unexpected neanderthal leap across the Pennines, lunch on Leeds. It is stock still: black, broad and stumpy. Don't turn your back on it, because the wide-spreading foliage is still thick enough to hide a Robin-on-the-run, especially if dressed, as I suppose he would be, in Sherwood green.

But for all its bull-like appearance, the geological wood-gout has set in. There are signs of overweight, a loss of grip. Three or four pit props support the outer branches. How long it will last no one can say, but Sherwood Forest will never be the same when it goes. A fence gives it space, because the weight of too many people crowding for photographs made it difficult for tap roots to get food from the soil.

Four children stand by the fence for fond parents to take a picture. They want the tree in it, but the children won't hold still, as children often won't, nor will they get close enough, so a certain amount of pushing is necessary, in the course of which I learn that their names are Scott, Lee, Shelley and Liza, Liza pronounced not as in the old

78

Nottingham Castle

days, to rhyme with miser, but as tweezer or geezer. They almost clamber on top of each other, until a snapshot satisfies those who think that Major Oak once concealed Robin and his Merry Muggers.

Forest-style beehive buildings, far enough from the oak tree not to offend its antique lineage, form the visitors' centre. There are toilets and a café, and an exhibition of maps, drawings and photographs showing the economic, political and natural history of the region. A bookshop stocks relevant publications, and school parties enjoy the Centre as an educational place as they run around with sketchpads and notebooks.

Put in a 10p piece and a machine will get Robin Hood to sing you a song. On the menu at the café there's Little John's Choice – hot cheese and mushroom roll served with garnish; Friar Tuck's Jacket Potato – with butter, cheese or savoury filling. Or you can munch Robin Hood's Favourite Baconburger in a sesame seed bap served with a garnish and sauces. A Longbow is a jumbo sausage in a long roll with onions and mustard. A Target Ring is a doughnut with jam. And of course for dessert there's Maid Marian's pippin pie, a wedge of apple pie served with cream. I don't know how long such convenience food would have let them pursue their energetic career of robbing and the redistribution of wealth (ha-ha!). Certainly, acorn bread and raw venison would have put them more in the mood.

On my way back to Major Oak a worried young man asks me if I have seen a little dark-haired boy who answers to the name of Martin. I say I'll look out for him. The loss rate must be high in this part of the county, because the track from Oak Tree to Tourist Centre makes a circuit, and it is easy to imagine some adventurous mite going under a fence and setting out on a vector of no return.

Lunch is eaten leaning against a fallen trunk some way from the loud and constant admiration of Major Oak. The distant movement of people is colourful, even picturesque, but I have misanthropically grown to like the peace and quiet among the oak trees, one of which looks as if it is in the grip of python coils, which turned to stone while someone chopped at them with an axe. Other oaks are upstanding, but died, like many people, on their feet. Some have been blasted again and again by lightning, and resemble ruined semaphore towers which signalled one bulletin of bad news too many. The gnarled branches of one blasted oak rise above silver birches, as if they have sucked it dry and are still in the process of reducing it to dust. In longevity the oak lost the fight to smaller fry. Summer dulls it all, and makes it sinister. Don't stare too long. The forest has most colour in autumn, when the ferns turn brown, and green is mixed with copper.

To push my journey on another stage it is necessary to refer to the compass, because with sore feet I can't afford to retrace my steps. A fringe benefit at the Visitors' Centre, before I leave, is that I can fill my flask at the watertap. Going through mixed wood and scrubland means ticking off paths that cross or branch so as to know my exact position on the map, navigating carefully now that there are no roads, railways or pylons as check points, or mansions on which to take bearings. The agricultural area of Nottinghamshire declined sixty-three per cent from 1801 to 1901, and still further since. The population of the county was 981,000 at the last census (most of it in urban settlements), whereas during my childhood it was about 700,000.

I'm walking through Budby South Forest, an unpopulated tract and an army training ground in two wars. Even before, the Sherwood Rangers and the South Nottinghamshire Hussars used it for tactical training at their annual camps. They probably still do. There were two territorial regiments of volunteer cavalry in the county, the Yeomanry formed in 1798, and the Hussars in 1794 in whose service an uncle of mine died during the Great War.

A heavy tank by the trackside is immobilised and ruined. A similar vehicle further on has been dug into sandy ground as a fixed gunnery point. Much of the forest is still War Office property, it seems, and some of the diverging paths display warnings to KEEP OUT. Red Army take note. Perhaps mines or unexploded shells are littered about. Trespassers will be mutilated.

Continual reference to the map makes me wonder what I look at yet don't see. My feet tread the solid landscape and it's easy to relate

Near Eastwood

the rise of land with the closing together of contour lines; a dark crest of woods to a small green shape. But I search the map and scrutinise the paysage with the feeling that something vital eludes me. I do not sufficiently belong to the land to know what it signifies, except at certain moments. I go my way, wondering whether possession of a map doesn't dull the senses, and deprive them of a fresh look at the country. The land goes dead at one moment, and comes to life the next, by some mysterious process that has nothing to do with me.

Two more tanks look as if they haven't heard the sound of their own engines for decades, but in my imagination the driver, captain, gunner and loader send out and finally get – death. They feel elation, then fear. They sweat, and are covered in dust. Petrol stench tells me of death by fire, the smell of burning rags on their backs. I see their faces, and think of each man's temperament, wondering about his family and where he came from, and of his childhood at school. One of my cousins died in a tank in North Africa.

At two o'clock I rest on dry grass by a hedge. The walk from Mansfield is harder than expected, though not because of broken terrain or much distance. One or two blisters can easily be walked into quiescence, but my right ankle is hard and swollen, and that seems to be another matter.

Thunder clatters like sticks in the distance. Clouds are on the boil, shades of dark grey steaming around in a mix. A damp breeze replaces warm stillness.

I get up so as to put in more mileage. A mechanical waterspray near the edge of a field emits a cloud of moisture that has been visible for some time, as if to encourage the gentle rain that now begins, the kind that seems determined to go on and, if possible, increase. My jacket is proof against it, and so is the hood which, pulled from the rear pocket, effectively cowls my head. The lark and the cuckoo make their noises and, while rain falls, the spraying machine drives a circular veil of water around the field, at one point inundating the land by which I descend, so that I wait till the contraption turns its attention to the interior of the field before going quickly by.

I intended exploring the Carburton and Clumber areas, but

tramping through soaked forests is not my idea of pleasure. I decide to make for Norton a few miles away, where Grange Farm does bed-and-breakfast. If the sky is dry in the morning I'll walk across the Dukeries to Retford. At least that's the idea, but the ridge around my ankle is iron-hard and hot. Perhaps it would have been more sensible to wear a pair of ordinary shoes instead of walking boots. I read somewhere that a few members of the British Army climbing team, on the 200-mile approach march to Mount Everest, wore plimsolls. I should have done the same.

After Lord Woodstock's plantation I take the lane to Norton by Hatfield Grange. In the village I ask a schoolgirl the way to Grange Farm, but she looks at me as if such a soaked figure might try to kidnap her. 'It's a place where they do bed-and-breakfast,' I add.

She steps back on hearing this probably obscene suggestion. She's only thirteen after all, but thinks the farm must be up *that* way. In a few minutes I arrive and, seeing two or three cars in the yard, assume the rooms are taken. Unwilling to walk anymore, I envisage a bus ride to Worksop or Mansfield.

A young bearded farmer answers the door. Yes, he thinks there is a vacancy. His wife confirms the fact, and shows me into a room with sufficient bedspace for a family. Mrs Palmer goes back to feeding the calves, and I have half an hour to unpack and change before coming down to the lounge for a Nottinghamshire-size teapot and a plate of biscuits.

Warm and dry, reclining in a padded armchair, with rain splattering at the other side of the window glass, is a sweet change from a bedraggled plodding of the footpaths. A fat business-like thrush digs a hapless worm out of the lawn, as if to join me in my snack. With X-ray eyes it must have waited hours for that worm to come within pecking range. Maybe it flies a regular aerial survey to find out if a new family has moved in.

Mrs Palmer doesn't do evening meals, so after a nap I get into boots and jacket and march a mile to the Greendale Oak in Cuckney village. In spite of rain the walk seems short, and I am soon downing a glass of vodka in the saloon bar. The meal begins with tinned grapefruit, followed by a plate of lamb chops and overdone

84

vegetables, ending with cheese and biscuits, and a cup of weak coffee – for the price of three pounds. The juke box bounces its music to a dance going on in the next room, which sounds a bit too much like the Surabaya Foxtrot to be endured. After a relaxing cigar I step back through the rain to my cushy billet at Grange Farm. The quicker I walk the less painful my ankle feels.

More tea and biscuits are brought to the living-room. I assume that a young man watching television is a son of the house, and too blasé to converse with passing travellers. In bed, to the gentle rapping of raindrops at the glass, I read of Alexander's army marching sixty miles a day towards the mountains of Central Asia.

Breakfast is taken with the man who was watching television last night. While pebbles of rain slash at the window we talk our way through a quantity of eggs and bacon, in which I discover that he is not the son of the house but works for the Ordnance Survey, marking in those buildings which are missing from the 1:50,000 maps. They are then plotted to twice the scale so that when his insertions are reduced, sufficient accuracy can be established. He uses a box sextant to measure angles, and for directions employs a prismatic compass of the army type. The age-old pacing system is considered accurate enough for distances, but on such wet days as this he might be tempted to work from the car, fixing buildings by triangulation, though I hope there's a compass deviation card stuck on his dashboard.

Asked how he obtained such interesting work, he tells me that he just applied for it. Had he done a degree in geography? Not at all. They trained him after he joined the organisation. Before that he worked for the Inland Revenue, but he likes the present occupation better, which is easy for me to understand. Grange Farm is a good base from which to reconnoitre the Dukeries area, and next week he hopes to go to Scotland. I show him my hand-held telescope with built-in compass, a device he hasn't seen before but which he thinks might be useful for his kind of work.

My ankle gave an uneasy time even in sleep, a reminder that it would still ache in the morning, so I decide to get on a bus to the nearest railway station, even if the rain stops. This means that I will miss viewing the noble houses of the Dukeries, most of which are closed to the public anyway. And to see the famous Greendale Oak – or what's left of it – I would have to trespass, because it is on private property and almost a kilometre from the public footpath.

The tree has a curious history. Last night's pub was named after it. No one knows how long it has stood, though for a long time the hollow trunk was propped up with chains and beams, looking much like a grand old soldier who had been through the wars. Life flickered longer than expected. Throsby the antiquarian wrote in 1797 that it was 'supposed to be upwards of 1,500 years old'. The first Duke of Portland said that he could drive a carriage through it, and in 1724 had an arch cut out of the trunk to prove that he could, an act which did no good for the tree's longevity. A cabinet he ordered to be made from the timber for the Countess of Oxford is perhaps lasting longer than the now jumbled heap of the tree.

Nor would I get to Clumber Park, where water creams over the lip of the weir by Carburton Bridge, and flows between serpentine gnarled roots of the trees. I must also forsake another call at my most favourite spot in this part of the world, Hardwick Grange, a village of homogeneous sandstone nineteenth-century estate houses. Being miles from the tourist run, there's no museum or tea house or church or souvenir shop. The end of Clumber Lake by which it stands is isolated and wood-lined and you drive far through the forest to reach it (use a map) and to get out to the south you need to go through a ford. In my novel *The Widower's Son*, the widower himself, Charlie Scorton, takes his son William there for walks on Sunday.

I pay Mrs Palmer the reasonable reckoning of five pounds, shoulder my pack, put up the hood of my jacket and set out for the village. A glass-framed timetable outside the shop seems the place to wait, but for some reason the stop is two hundred yards beyond. When the bus goes by, the driver pulls up on seeing me wave, and we are soon charging on full headlights, such rain falling that the wheels create a bow wave on our way through Warsop.

86

The Major Oak

Clumber Park

Everything looks drenched and miserable compared to the last few days, especially the few miles of ribbon development before Mansfield. The Woodhouse is spectacularly dreary, and reminds me of when George Fox the Quaker came this way in 1648. In Nottingham he interrupted the preacher in his pulpit and was thrown into 'a nasty stinking prison; the smell whereof got so into my nose and throat that it very much annoyed me'. He was kept there some time, and on his release came to preach in Mansfield Woodhouse, '. . . but the people fell upon me in a great rage, struck me down, and almost stifled and smothered me, and I was cruelly beaten and bruised by them with their hands, Bibles and sticks. Then they haled me out, though I was hardly able to stand, and put me into the stocks, where I sate some hours; and they brought dog-whips and horse-whips, threatening to whip me. After some time, they had me before the magistrate, at a knight's house, where there were many great persons; who, seeing how evilly I had been used, after much threatening set me at liberty. But the rude people stoned me out of the town for preaching the word of life to them.'

The goodhearted bus driver takes me half a mile beyond his Mansfield terminus so that I can get on the Nottingham coach without being drenched. All the way there, by our zigzag route, there's no break in the sky. It's impossible to go through the middle of Nottingham, even though the rain has all but stopped, without calling at the secondhand bookshop on Heathcote Street, from which place a heavy tome on geomorphology adds an extra few pounds to my pack. I go through the new shopping centre to the station, and on the train calculate that the four-day trek of fifty miles has cost £46, from London back to London, including bus, bed, board and all expenses.

THE COUNTY

After a spell in Nottingham I take a trip to Skegness, eighty miles away on the Lincolnshire coast, because it has long been known as 'Nottingham-on-Sea', and a book about the county would not be complete without the record of a visit there. You can even see Tennyson's birthplace at Somersby on the way.

Leland in 1540 suggested that the original Skegness was a walled town with its own harbour, destroyed by the encroaching sea. In the nineteenth century fishermen lived there in cabins, beside a hotel and one thatched house, and the place had a population of about five hundred. Nottingham people call it 'Skeggy', which is perhaps as close as you can get to the original Danish of 'Skaeggi'. The Rev. Mackenzie E. C. Walcott, in his book *The East Coast of England* (1861), described the area somewhat purplishly:

'There are no rocks here, no bleak cliffs against which the wild blue billow leaps up in thunder, but there are little bays, low points, and marshy reaches, acres overgrown with short grass, sand-banks and rushes, lonely spots and bleak wastes, which the sea birds haunt, and love to skim over with their hoarse cries, melancholy pipe, and flashing wing: yet the sight is even grander than that of an iron coast. There is the vast ocean with its millions of restless waves, heaving with an eternal wail, as century after century it sobs against the sea wall, or bursts and booms in thunder upon the shore, and yet it cannot cross the low barrier that separates it from the inland; at other times it is rippling over with the tremulous emotion of a thousand sparkling diamond points.' In fact the sea defences broke

Skeggy

down in the storms of 1953, and caused much devastation in the low-lying farmland behind.

In 1873 a branch line was opened from Boston to Grimsby, and the first railway trips were run from Nottingham to Skegness. The rise of the place was due to the exertions and investments of the Earl of Scarborough, and now it's a town of thirteen thousand people, flat, nondescript but with pleasant residential streets open to sea breezes from a seemingly immense horizon. Inland are Tennyson's 'wide-winged sunsets of the misty marsh'.

When I was four I went on a day trip with my parents. Wandering away from the beach, I got lost, and was eventually found on the steps of the town hall waving a piece of stick in time to some tune in my head. My sister, throwing sand in the air at the joy of being by the sea, did not know that the last jug of tea was underneath. No wonder they never took us again.

When I was nine my mother wangled me a fortnight at Poor Boys Camp, set in fact in a large house. We played in a billiard hall in the garden when it rained, hammering a piano or skimming through a shelf of bound Penny Dreadfuls. Someone taught me to play draughts. We wore a kind of uniform for quick identification in case any of us absconded – or got lost – but had fun turning the grey felt hats into the headgear of Napoleon. We were walked to nearby hills blackberrying, though we weren't allowed to eat the fruit, which was taken back to the house and made into jam for the teachers who looked after us. At a concert party on the pier I felt afraid of water swirling under the floor.

It's hard to relate to such a time, driving there on a Saturday in high summer. A dozen diminutive donkeys on the beach give rides for 25p each. The scene is rather old-fashioned, with its wide sands, and (not a very good season) sparse occupants. But then, it takes little to make a beach look old-fashioned. Maybe it's the kind of people. The reason there are so few for a July day is, I am told by the man at the car park, because it is 'the change over' – a Saturday when people leave, and those who are coming for the following week have not yet arrived.

The beach is relatively clean except for the occasional donkey turds, and those which indicate that a horse has passed that way. Looking back from the sea's edge there's the Ferris Wheel, Swing Boats, Helter Skelter and various other sick-making structures on which people are enjoying themselves.

The Golden Sands of Skegness, as the posters say, never change, but the pier is broken now, the end piece a kind of shabby rig supporting a few rooms and the remains of a tower. A man sells popcorn, and music blares from the arcades. Walking through the town at midday, the *Nottingham Evening Post* is on sale. There are tat shops, cafés (friendly flies around the trash basket outside), fish and chip places, seafood bars, and tuckshops selling whipped cream, candyfloss, doughnuts, slushburgers, hot dogs, milk shakes and coffee to take away. To shake the stuff around into a trifle there's the Ghost Train to Hell (20p per person), electronic horse racing, kiddie rides, video, twist, waltz, gallopers, dodgems, skyride, flying saucers, jungle rides, zyklon and pirate ship. The Death Valley voice from a bingo arcade sounds like the countdown into penury.

Skeggy is predominantly a resort of the middle-aged and elderly. Either they can't afford Benidorm, or they want to come back to the favourite venues of their youth – maybe both. In 1964 a survey showed that seventy-four per cent of visitors were family groups. Not much Mr and Mrs Smithing here, you might think. At one time the railway was threatened with closure, since only eighteen per cent of visitors arrived by it, but for the moment the station is where it always was – half a mile west of the clock tower.

All the white skins and countable ribs and wobbling bosoms from Nottingham and neighbouring places are here. Along the seafront is the Dirk and Dagger, the Parade Hotel, the Promenade Snack Bar, Swimming Pool, Compass Restaurant (mind where you go). At the north end of town notices in boarding house windows advertise bed and breakfast for as little as £5·50.

You can tell men's ages to the nearest decade by the amount of clothes they wear in hot weather. The very young are naked to the waist, many sporting elaborate tattoos on chests and arms. The next

96

Skegness

stage up is a vest, then a shirt. Above forty, a jacket is usually in order. At fifty a sweater or a cardigan as well. The old wear a tie, and the eldest a hat and even a raincoat.

But against all the odds a man between the age of thirty and forty goes by whistling a piercing melodious tune which I can't for a moment recognise, though it is certainly familiar. He has a thin red face and good features, and short wavy hair turning grey. Going from the quiet boarding house area in the northern part of town towards the noisy promenade by the clock tower, he walks as if he has someone special to meet. Maybe he arrived an hour ago and, having settled his room and changed into grey trousers, checked jacket, open-necked shirt and well polished brown shoes, is losing no time about it, but will entertain himself and anyone who cares to listen on the way.

You heard much more whistling at one time, but the art is dying. Anyone musical can whistle, though there's more in the north than in the south of England. They don't need lessons as with a proper instrument, but to them the result is obviously divine. You can tell by the expressions on their faces. In my day men were the great whistlers, while women usually hummed.

Someone else on hearing the man remarks caustically that bird seed must be cheap at Skeggy these days. He whistles like an artist, happy being by the sea on a day seen mostly on posters at dingy railway stations in the depths of winter. If I had my way I would crown him King of Skegness for a season – except for my annoyance at not being able to recognise the tune he whistles.

Then I remember being on parade in the RAF, with the station band playing during a ceremonial inspection. The commanding officer walked along open-order ranks and looked fiercely at each man's buttons, boots and shaven chin, while the idiotic tune of 'After the ball is over . . . . .' brayed out to the leaden Lancashire sky.

The whistling grows dim and the man vanishes on his way to God knows where, while I wander through the grid-patterned streets towards the main drag. The working model of a toy steam engine in a shop window is something I haven't seen since the days when

98

my father bought a kit and tried to build one. His smile of triumph when by handiwork, know-how, fuel and water he got it going on the kitchen table, stays with me. Wheels turned and the piston went in and out, under the admiring silence of us four children.

For lunch I have ravioli, followed by roast lamb, then jam roll and custard and a pot of tea – a real Nottingham dinner – served by Virginia, whose name is written on the bill of four pounds. Outside, enormous quantities of chips are being consumed. Scores of people sit in the sun by pubs and cafés, eating from plastic plates to the jangling zombie-like beat of music from an arcade. If you live in Nottingham you don't need an interpreter at Skeggy. I imagine there's a toll gate half-way between city and coast through which they only let people who have the right accent and features.

Sooner or later, enjoying it though I think I am, I cut and run. The intensity gets too much and, on the outskirts of the town I set the car's snout towards the sparkling Trent and the emerald green of Sherwood, to do a clock-circuit of the county and rope in more of my favourite haunts.

If one visits Skegness in Lincolnshire because the living spirit of Nottingham resides there for much of the year, one comes to Crich in Derbyshire because the spirit of the dead from the Great War is commemorated in the monument to the Sherwood Foresters, which makes it as much part of Nottinghamshire as the county in which it stands.

On the way there a roadside notice says: 'Derbyshire supports nuclear free zones'. Perhaps the Crich monument to the memory of men killed in the Great War helped towards this frame of mind, though Nottinghamshire, bloody-minded as usual, boasts no such notice.

Seen from the Heights of Abraham above Matlock, Crich Tower, on its solitary limestone cliff, looks like a rocket ready for blast-off, as if in spite of all its good intentions Derbyshire has been secretly preparing a space programme and will any day astonish the world. From

Skegness

Crich Monument itself, nearly a thousand feet above sea level, you can on a day of good visibility (with binoculars) pick out Belvoir Castle thirty-three miles away, and Lincoln Cathedral, at over forty miles.

A tower has been on Crich Stand for centuries, though the present structure was built in 1851. The dome of a hill on which it is built (on the ruins of three previous towers) is a geological curiosity, being formed from limestone forced up through later strata by volcanic action. In 1882 a landslip altered the shape of the hill, and did much damage at its foot.

A man brings the key from a house nearby as soon as he sees my car on the approach road, and opens the door to the tower so that I can climb the staircase to the top. It is a good site for the Sherwood Foresters' memorial, looking as it does over both counties. The railings around it were presumably taken away for scrap during the Second World War. The inscription over the doorway reads: 'To the memory of 11,409 men of all ranks of The Sherwood Foresters (Nottinghamshire and Derbyshire Regiment) who gave their lives for their King and their Country in the Great War 1914–1919, and in honour of the 140,000 of their Comrades who served during the War in 32 Battalions of the Regiment, this Monument is gratefully erected by the People of the Counties of Nottingham and Derby. To remind us of their sacrifice and our Duty.'

On the path leading to the tower is a memorial to Sir Horace Smith-Dorrien, Colonel of the Regiment 1905–30. The memorial was opened in 1923, and homage continues with a service every year on the first Sunday in July, a date as near to 1 July 1916 as possible.

On that day, in the Battle of the Somme, three battalions of the regiment were practically wiped out, mostly to the north of Gommecourt in Picardy. Exhausted after a week's labouring to bring supplies to the front-line trenches, and overburdened with up to seventy pounds of equipment, the 5th and 7th Battalions got out of their muddy trenches at seven o'clock and advanced at a slow walk towards the German lines 500 yards away. They fell by the score to machine guns and artillery.

The dead would not have forgiven had they come back to life, most of them even unable to get through the barbed wire entanglements, which they were told had been previously cut away by gunfire. The wounded – some of them – were grateful for survival. The scathless were no doubt subdued, but no one really forgave the incompetence. Many houses in the two counties had their blinds drawn during those early July days of 1916.

The enormity of the losses rankled even during the Second World War, in which conflict the 2nd Battalion of the Sherwood Foresters lost 359 men in six years, proving that they fought just as well, but more wisely.

Apart from the 150,000 referred to on the War Memorial, many served or became casualties in yeomanry regiments, or the artillery or the engineers, or in other fighting units of the Navy or Flying Corps.

On August Bank Holiday Sunday 1923 thousands of people came on foot, by bicycle, and by motor car, from all parts of the two counties. Special buses ran from Ambergate station. General Smith-Dorrien, one of the better generals of the War, was brought back in April 1915 after falling foul of the commander-in-chief, Sir John French, and put in command of a Home Army.

He spoke on behalf of his 'beloved regiment'. Among the spectators were numbers of wounded who had come by charabanc and made their painful way up to the memorial. 'Whosoever leads such a life,' the inscription says, 'need not care upon how short warning it be taken from him.' It was, the *Derby Advertiser* said: 'a service of unforgettable solemnity'.

From the top of the tower the wind blows so strongly that I don't stay long. The hills of South Derbyshire, patched with straight-sided woodland, and the pit villages of Nottinghamshire to the east seem denuded of inhabitants. There are spits of rain in the wind, and the man is waiting to lock the door and go back home with his key.

George V visited the Western Front after the German offensive of 21 March 1918, and inspected the 2nd Battalion of the Sherwood Foresters which had been almost wiped out. 'You must have seen some hard fighting in your time, ' the King remarked to one soldier. 'Yes, sir,' the soldier replied, 'but this last lot was the bloody limit!'

102

Skegness

In 1918 several thousand recruits were camped in Welbeck Park, and General Sir John Maxwell inspected them in the riding school, accompanied by the Duke of Portland. Sir John asked one of the youths if he was looking forward to going to France, and the youth replied that he was not. The General asked why, to be told: 'The Germans are big men and I be afeered of 'em!' The rest of the parade burst out laughing, and the General saw that it was a joke, and that the youth had been put up to it by his mates, because the Duke of Portland said that the recruits in this batch were big Nottinghamshire lads who wouldn't be afraid of anybody.

From Crich I motor around the oval clockface of the Nottinghamshire map, a long but by no means unsmiling face because the weather is improving.

All English counties are unique, otherwise they would not have different names. On the other hand the only lasting definition of Nottinghamshire is that it is entirely surrounded by land – though that alone does not make it unique, because twenty English counties have access to the sea, while twenty do not. Instead of a coastline Nottinghamshire has the banks of the Trent, a river second only in length to the Severn among free-flowing English waterways. A hundred and forty-seven miles long, the river is clear and the current rapid by the time it enters Nottinghamshire, whose soil it washes for the next eighty miles.

To the west of the river much of Sherwood Forest still exists, if the woods of the Dukeries are included. The frontier of the county wiggles for 180 miles, half of which length goes along streams and rivers. It is a county, after all, and not a country.

Being neither north nor south, Nottinghamshire is defined more by history than by spectacular topography. It is the key to the country, geographically, mentally and strategically. In the Civil War the area was fought for tenaciously by Cavalier and Roundhead, on the premise that if Nottingham and the Trent valley was lost, so was the cause. Much skirmishing occurred, but that which took place nearly two centuries later during the industrial revolution caused

104

more smoke than broken heads, though there were more British soldiers in the region holding down the people than there were fighting the French army in Spain.

The way Nottingham goes, so does the country, but Nottingham often and wisely decides to go nowhere, and so stays idiosyncratic and independent. Miners in the recent coalstrike kept on working, tragic though this seemed to many. Whereas tactics are suitable for some areas, Nottinghamshire requires diplomacy, and that doesn't always work.

A county is safest without well-defined frontiers to hide behind, providing people retain their own opinions, and an intimate knowledge of the space within which they live. Rivers don't protect nor hills deter, and only a unique spirit is proof against extinction.

West Nottinghamshire rises into the hills of Derbyshire, and to the south it blends with Leicestershire. The northern speartip melts innocuously into the flat land which indicates that the Humber isn't far away. To the east lies Lincolnshire, a mere proxy for a Nottinghamshire coastline. Between these foreign borders there is sufficient space for independent characteristics to develop.

After Crich I go nonstop via Alfreton and Tibshelf to Hardwick Hall, home of the Great Bess, still inside Derbyshire, but close to home ground and more than worthy of a look even if only to compare it with Wollaton Hall.

A list of opening times tells me that the Hall is closed, however, and that even the grounds won't open till twelve, an hour away. The house is partly visible over walls too high to climb, and there are picturesque ruins opposite with a notice saying that you must not approach because they are extremely dangerous. The M1 motorway is down the hill and a thousand yards to the west, and even the stateliest of mansions is not spared the traffic's growl. Travelling down the motorway from Sheffield, on the other hand, you get a wonderful view of the Hall, providing you dare take your eyes for a second off the perilous road.

Bess of Hardwick was a squire's daughter, who married four times and on each occasion more grandly. Out of her riches she built the Hall, which cost the same as the one at Wollaton, as if both

Belvoir Castle

proprietors saw it on the same shelf and wanted one each.

Over the bleak agricultural uplands I drive to Cresswell Crags, a glen with Nottinghamshire on one side and Derbyshire on the other. The senses are split between a scene of beauty and a catastrophic lack of silence. Laden coal lorries use a minor road running along one side of the glen, a road so narrow that traffic lights are set up to control the flow. The best views are from that side, but it is hard to stand there without wondering whether the next moment is going to be your last. Nevertheless, my senses negating such annoyances, the sound of running water is pleasant, and delight predominates. A footpath leads from the Visitors' Centre, also closed, by a babble of rust-coloured water. Another arm of the stream is choked with moss. Beyond the trees a dam has created a lake whose length divides the two counties.

The whole glen is bordered by magnesian limestone cliffs, with vegetation in their clefts, and hazel, ash, maple, oak and alder trees lining the tops. Looking ahead, through the glen and at no great distance, are the outworks of a colliery, and an enormous spoilbank hundreds of yards long through which a long streak of reddish sandstone goes, lending another kind of drama to the countryside.

Cresswell Crags is a miniature Dovedale, without the subtle windings of the Dove. Watercourses streak through mudflats where the lake has become slightly drained. Such delicate miniaturism was not created by man, but simply worn down by him.

Trees rustle in the wind, and the glen becomes a world of its own, cut off from the surrounding countryside. There's something protective yet eerie about it, the place at one time having been a refuge for Robin Hood and his companions, in the days when the forest of Sherwood extended well beyond Nottinghamshire. The hollowed bolt-holes among the rocks on the northern side have such names as Robin Hood's Cave and Little John's Cavern.

The place is riddled with caves, and explorations in 1870 disclosed the remains of Palaeolithic Man. Human bones of the early Stone Age were found, as well as weapons, and some carvings. There was evidence that at least two glacial periods passed over the area, and that thousands of years intervened between periods of habitation.

A moorhen pecks at a Coke tin in the bulrushes. Teasel, nettles and ragged robin line the banks. Scenery seems better when walking back towards the east, a pleasant stroll between wooded limestone heights. There's a line of silver birch, with no coalmines or buildings visible, though the rumble of a coal lorry, and the whine of a jet fighter, deny the illusion of peace.

Worksop is five miles away, along a typical woodland Dukeries road. Mysterious gates are guarded by grey-stoned lodges which, with their small windows, look the epitome of cosiness.

When the war began in 1939 scores of doubledecker buses evacuated children from Nottingham. The four of our family each carried a gasmask and a paperbag of belongings. Only a baby had stayed behind.

None of us knew that we would be coming back. We imagined that our parents would be buried when the house collapsed under a bomb, and thought little more about it. After all, it was our first long bus ride, and in Sherwood Forest we joked about being ambushed by Robin Hood and robbed of our spending money. Many were singing, and some were sick out of the windows.

At Worksop we were sifted through and taken to different houses. I went to Sandhill Street, and Mrs Coutts gave me a basin of beef stew then sent me to bed for the afternoon because she thought I needed to recover from the shock of leaving home, whereas I wanted to get out and explore the new streets.

During the three months of my stay I shared a double bed with another boy in the house which was not too different from the one I had left. We were looked after like their own children, and I was bemused, to say the least, when our parents, having got bored when no bombing occurred, fetched us back to Nottingham.

I park my car near the market, and look down the straight main street which has altered little except that the Gaiety Cinema is closed. The busy thoroughfare is gritty and homely. Sandhill Street has been obliterated, and the town seems less prosperous and lively than in 1939, certainly less exciting.

The Old Lock-up at Tuxford

I was to make Worksop the town of Ashfield in my novel *The Widower's Son*. The Couttses' son was a boy soldier, like William Scorton in the novel, though their circumstances were entirely different.

Later during the war I would bike the twenty-seven miles from Nottingham to visit Mrs Coutts, but we had little to say. After half an hour I'd set off home, enjoying my solitary ride across the county. A bicycle's radius of action pushed the horizon steadily outwards, took me through strange towns and villages when there were no signposts, nor proper maps in the shops. It was terra incognita, in more ways than one, exploring the wartime lanes and roads. The city was left behind much sooner than it is now, and it was so rare to see a motor car that some kids passed the time writing down the number of any that passed. Food was scarce. The few cafés often closed as soon as they ran out of supplies. You carried whatever you could get from home, though there was neither hardship nor complaint, since everyone was better fed than before the war.

I get into my car and head for Blyth, which has a neat and pretty main street, or maybe it only seems so after Worksop. There are two hotels, and a combined bakery and delicatessen which I make use of for lunch. Parking is easy along a stretch of greensward, because though it's the main Nottingham–Doncaster road, traffic has been drained off by the motorway.

I go through Bawtry to Finningley at the top of the county, so far north I'm almost in Yorkshire, and reach for my passport in case they've claimed UDI since I last heard the news. If that were the case I suppose they'd have Braine for Prime Minister, Herriot as Minister of Health, Storey in the Home Office, Keith Waterhouse for Culture, Barstow for Defence and Willis Hall at the Foreign Office. Mercer would have been Prime Minister, but unfortunately he's no longer with us. Come home, boys, all is forgiven.

The Blaxton Café gives bed and breakfast just north of Finningley on the main road, but the only thing special about the place is the aerodrome, a famous RAF bomber base during the war. From a lay-by it looks very spick and permanent as I observe it through binoculars to see what the old mob is up to.

110

The barbed point of flat Notts points towards the soft underbelly of the Humber, so I turn east and then south for Gainsborough, marking out bed and breakfast places as overnight stops for a Trent Walk which I have in mind. South of Stockwith the rhythmical bash of oil pumps in the fields tells me that no sod is being left unturned for when the North Sea runs dry of its convertible currency. After the miners' strike I suppose new priorities arise. But the closure of pits will be seen as nothing less than tragic in the years to come when it is discovered that there isn't so much oil after all.

Clouds play cat and mouse with the sun as I head through Newark on to the Fosse Way, passing Flintham Lane where I spent a wet week under canvas with the ATC, in attendance at nearby Syerston aerodrome.

Lower down the Fosse, RAF Newton stretches to my right, a Polish aerodrome during the war, which is why there's a large Polish community in Nottingham. One of their pilots gave me my first flight in 1943, and in the mess I ate my first 'foreign' meal, which is why I still like food from that part of the world.

Going through Bingham, and then along the lanes, I get to Langar, the birthplace of Samuel Butler (1835–1902) and immortalised, if that word can possibly be used about a well-hidden village which ignores him, in his novel *The Way of All Flesh* as Battersby-on-the-Hill. The red-bricked ivy-clad rectory is still there.

I didn't know of his existence during the time I worked at the nearby aerodrome on air traffic control in 1945. Opposite the runways the hangars of the A. V. Roe factory turned out York airliners. Lincoln bombers had previously been made, some of which, never to be used, were parked on the dispersal points.

In those days I took a bus to the city centre at seven o'clock, then boarded a works bus to the aerodrome thirteen miles away. I unlocked the tower (the door approached by a flight of outside steps) and made a pot of tea, taking a mug to the flying control officer who slept downstairs. My day's duty began by getting weather reports from all over the country and plotting them on a meteorological chart.

Though my wages were almost halved to when I worked on a

Skegness

capstan lathe I was happy during the eight months as a temporary civil servant with the Ministry of Aircraft Production. I had already enlisted, but was not called up until the following May.

The aerodrome had ceased to be operational, though the RAF still manned the telephone exchange. I listened to the football match against the Moscow Dynamo team on an old R-1155 Marconi, and hoped the Russians would win, much to the chagrin of the RAF corporal, who admitted however that they had to win, otherwise Stalin would have them shot.

My duties included guiding aircraft into dispersal points with two tennis bats, and occasionally climbing on to the wing of an Avro Anson with a starting handle to prime the first engine. Or I would sit in the turret of a chequerboard caravan on the end of the runway signalling aircraft to land or take off. Something different happened every day, and I can only marvel (though I didn't then) at the responsibilities given to a seventeen-year-old.

I park my car by the tower. The place has been through many vicissitudes, and now belongs to a parachute club. The room I kept watch from, windows all round, is the club lounge. Nobody asks questions when I go downstairs and get a cup of tea at the bar. A young man tells me he's writing a history of the aerodrome, and the information that I once worked there isn't much of a contribution to his research because I can't mention squadron numbers or the names of commanding officers – only that the test pilot of the time, Squadron Leader Peter Field-Richards, took me for a flight over Nottingham in a York.

A group (or should I say a stick?) of parachutists walk to a Cessna parked on the perimeter. The black-and-white club cat stalks with enormous self-confidence by a notice saying: 'Positively no dogs allowed'.

There's a holiday atmosphere about the place. Thousands of tiny birds cross the sky, the whole cloud making a sort of pterodactyl head and tail which seems miles long – a kite of birds weaving and waving towards the wooded escarpment of Plungar.

The Cessna comes back over the airfield, and when the first

parachutist tumbles out into space a man behind me says to his little boy:

'That's *your* muther!'

Most of the candidates for the test seem to be women, and the cutest parachutist I've ever seen, complete with flowing hair, makes a correct landfall, and walks towards the control tower with the white billowing chute gathered to her bosom, and smiling nervously as her boyfriend waits to immortalise the moment with a camera.

I cross the Fosse Way once more towards Nottingham, and call at the Holme Pierrepont watersports area, where a mile-long stretch of water by the Trent is sufficient for a flying boat to land on. There's a kiosk for tea, and a quiet corner in which to park and fall asleep for half an hour.

A few miles west on fast roads get me to the Hemlock Stone, near Bramcote. Up hill from the parking place, a fifty-foot-high mass of red sandstone rock – looking fairly black by now – is surrounded by railings to prevent people either chiselling their initials on it, or sawing chunks off and carrying it away bit by bit.

The troubled sky is streaked with bits of white, as if after a cosmic dogfight, and the first view of the Hemlock Stone rising out of the greenery is like suddenly coming on a dark misshapen glove-puppet of huge proportions that has been involved in a tragic accident. It used to be more isolated, and thus more dignified in appearance, but now there are houses nearby.

The Stone has stood for thousands of years, and will no doubt last thousands more, unless a nuclear hit scorches it to the roots and pushes the dust five hundred feet underground.

Like a gnarled but grand old man – seventy feet round and weighing over two hundred tons – it looks mutely from a sea of green over the mixed countryside of the two counties. As children we believed that the ancient Brits danced widdershins around it with ivy-juice dribbling down their beards. The Druids no doubt made use of it in their rites, and up to the end of the sixteenth century a fire was annually lit on Beltane Eve. The word *beltane* comes from Baal, and *teine* means fire, suggesting that the Celts were also worshippers

114

Skegness

Skegness

of Baal, and lasted longer at their malpractices because Elijah the Tishbite wasn't able to deal with them as he did with the Baalim on Mount Carmel, on which altar 'the fire of the Lord fell, and all was consumed, the sacrifice, wood, stones, dust, and water'.

The Hemlock Stone inspires poetic speculation. To run seven times around it was said to be a sure cure for rheumatism, though I never met anyone who would swear to such an effect. It was a landmark to cycle to from Nottingham. The Stone was more isolated in 1902 when Paul Morel in *Sons and Lovers* walked there from Eastwood with Miriam and other friends, a round trip through Ilkeston of about sixteen miles. Paul was disgusted at the fact that visitors had carved their initials on it. So did Byron scratch his, on the wall of the dungeon in which the prisoner of Chillon had resided for six years, but in his case they put a little frame around it.

Nearer the base of the Hemlock Stone is a kind of striated red sandstone, and people of these days have been over the railings and aerosolled their initials on it, the only virtue of this modern invention being that it will probably fade quicker than anything else.

Further up the hill, through a wood of small oaks, walking in the silence between evergreens and ferns, I emerge into the space of a trigonometrical point. A wide expanse of green fields and farmhouses can be seen, and much spattering of late-nineteenth-century conurbation. In 1940 the Home Guard held tactical exercises around these hills, and an officer standing by the stone had a copy of the relevant Ordnance Survey sheet folded into a smart mapcase. While he discussed matters with his staff I edged as close as I dared to look at it, for I had never seen such a map of an area I knew.

Looking as far as the horizon with binoculars I pick out remnants of mills and chimneys, cooling towers and houses, as well as the occasional steeple, and the distant power station. There are many new dwellings, and an occasional patch of greensward between each planned (and unplanned) spread. Below the top of the hill is Field Farm, and Stanton Iron Works just inside Derbyshire. Trowel Hall, a mid-Victorian Elizabethan-style house, is partly visible.

A man comes up through the wood with a dog, followed by an old bloke pushing a pram with a baby in it. Time to go back to Nottingham. It's been a long day getting around the oval clock face of the county. A deep pink band obscures the horizon as I drive into the city.

RIVER TRENT

The refreshment room on platform four of the Midland Station in Nottingham is, in decor, like something from the year 1900. Flowers hang at the windows, and there are furnishings to match. Maybe the food is different to what it was – I imagine the tea certainly is – but the atmosphere is of another and more agreeable age. The spacious room seems like one of the few peaceful places left in the world.

The train takes me to Long Eaton, to begin my walk of the River Trent from where it enters Nottinghamshire to where it leaves the county, connecting in a trek of several pedestrian stages many places I know, and some that I do not. The serpentine course of the river covers about eighty miles and, disregarding the misgivings of my feet, I set off.

I hadn't intended walking Nottinghamshire to the extent of covering 130 miles in two separate hikes, but I feel there's no other way to see it properly. The method is sufficiently different to make it interesting. As a youth I did thousands of miles on the bicycle, and would never have dreamed of walking unless I had to – though I had to very often. Walking was common. Before the war we couldn't afford bus fares, or we had better things to buy than transport, and during the war buses stopped so early that every Saturday night I walked four miles back from my girlfriend's house. Acquiring a bike and suddenly speeding along at ten or twenty miles an hour opened a new dimension of existence – of time, that is. I was thirty-three before I was able to buy a car and drive at over seventy, but each increase in speed meant seeing less, hence back to Shanks's pony for a few days travel along the course of the Trent.

Except for a stretch of nature reserve to the left of the line near Attenborough, the nine-mile rail journey from Nottingham is all warehouses, lorry parks, store hangars, dumping grounds and modern factories. Conurbation spreads like the blight, but I am part of it, and glad to be alive, so there's no complaining, since such a blight produces the comforts I enjoy.

Some English railway stations are united in nostalgia by smells so subtle that you can't put a name to them. At Long Eaton I detect the lost odour of gas lamps. Train smoke seems to linger. Disinfectant impregnates floors and wood fittings. Maybe only those over fifty notice it.

I walk down steps and through a few streets, the town edge marked by Lock Lane Level Crossing. The hedgerows beyond are rich in poppies, and purple-headed thistles as big as artichokes. Tufted vetch varies the scene, with white campion, buttercups, forget-me-nots, daisies, elderberry and brambles, and a snake of (unused) toilet paper draped over a hawthorn bush.

The settlement of Trent Lock is overshadowed by the cooling towers of a power station across the river, but it falls from the radar screen as I approach the dockyard and mooring area for boats, until only the densely wooded banks are visible. A gentle splashing comes from the lock over the Erewash Canal where it joins the river, a prevailing sound surrounding the Navigation and Steam Boat Inns. Both are enclosed by trees so that it's easy to imagine their gardens fully occupied in summer.

In the early nineteenth century enormous quantities of coal were transported by the Erewash Canal for shipment to the Trent, and on via Gainsborough to the Humber for coastwise distribution, Trent Lock being a major communications focus.

A yellow and blue barge called the *Phantom* chugs placidly upriver. The *Black Pug* is firmly moored, and a notice informs me that the bank is for private fishing by order of the Long Eaton Victoria Angling Society, while a British Waterways board states that HORSE RIDING, MOTORCYCLING, CYCLING IS PROHIBITED ON THIS TOWPATH.

A bee guzzles on the flowers of a dog rose. The *Gay Dolphin* hasn't

122

had a lick of paint for fifty years. The *Fly* of Nottingham and the *Madonna* of Hull languish in dock. All sorts and sizes of boats are moored along the banks: the *Misty*, the *Magpie*, the *Humdinger*, the *Innaminute* and the *Golden Gleam*. The green of sheep meadows is enriched by nine-tenths cumulus cloud, and the river snakes so much that you're never bored by a straight bit. A rifle range marked on the map produces no clatter of bullets.

A neck of land separates the river and an expanse of water created from worked-out gravel quarries, now a convoluted lake dotted with green islands and forming the Attenborough Nature Reserve. Overgrown banks make a home for swans and waterfowl after long flights from Spitzbergen.

Meadows across the river are speckled with cattle and sheep, Gotham Hills and the heights of Clifton in the background. Barton Ferry no longer operates, but as a youth I rode out from Nottingham over the toll bridge (Ha'penny Bridge), down through Clifton Grove to Barton-in-Fabis (Barton-in-the-Beans), then across the fields to be rowed over the river by an old man for a fee of twopence. With a map and a book on wild flowers in my bag, there seemed no greater contrast than that between an express train smoking in the distance and, on the bank I had just left, a pristine harebell hiding from the sun.

On a summer's evening I'd sometimes be the only passenger in his boat, and he rowed me across in silence, maybe wishing for more passengers, while my eyes were fixed on the other side. I pedalled the nine miles home, exercise soothing to the soul after the day's work.

Barton Island seems as far from the city as it is possible to get, surrounded by greenery, flanked by the river and the undisturbed lake of the nature reserve. The Trent looks lush and tropical, like some steamy bayou-tributary of the Mississippi. Vegetation and trees come down to the edge, tall bulrushes going into it on the other side, like a swamp. I imagine a crocodile or alligator wading out to get the lazy and inoffensive swimmer. His girlfriend on the bank calls for him to come back. The sun is shining and the water is blue around his white skin, but he doesn't hear. He thinks she must be joking, when he does. Alligators in the Trent? By then it is too late.

Several bungalows, and the headquarters of the Beeston Sailing Club, appear on the opposite bank, reflected in still water among the trees, fitting in with the scenery and contributing to the sleepy atmosphere.

A riverbank walk means there are no hills to descend. The Trent is ninety feet above sea level when it enters the county, and fifteen when it leaves, so you go downhill, if it can be called that, at the rate of a foot every mile. At Beeston Lock boats are moored by the score. Trees sleave the footpath as I approach the houses, and on emerging from the bushes a perfume of roses greets me from the pretty bungalow gardens.

The opposite shore is flat, then rises steeply wooded up to and almost enclosing the rambling establishment of Clifton Hall. The nearby Grove was one of my courting haunts. I cycled at speed along the avenue of lime trees, swerving to avoid ruts and roots. Or I scrambled down the banks between the trees, holding on to bushes to avoid falling, to swim from a narrow ledge by the water. I remember the icy flow one April when I was sixteen. Sometimes I would go there with a girl so that we could find a place and be undisturbed.

In the village there was a certain cottage garden where tea had been served for decades. Paul Morel in *Sons and Lovers* took Clara Dawes there, after he had more or less broken with his girlfriend Miriam. They scrambled down through the foliage to the swiftly flowing Trent, and later went on to the village. 'The old lady at whose home they had tea was roused into gaiety by them.' That must have been around 1910, and I went first in the early forties, so that perhaps the woman who served us was the daughter of she who had served Lawrence and his companion. The village is now lost among acres of postwar houses and the buildings of a college.

I separate from the river and make my way through streets to the Boat and Horseman where, for a pound, I lunch in the crowded yard on a cheese cob and a pint of shandy. Back by the weir a young biker is zooming and zigzagging across a field, threading under pylons, going far and coming back again, doing stunts and wheelies like a

Power

Cavalier trying to break in a recalcitrant horse for the delectation of his friends. It's a kind of bike ballet, without music except for the varying rhythms of the engine. I am too mesmerised at his daring to applaud, though he deserves it, but my stare breaks when he is thrown off and goes scooting across the grass. I fancy I hear his laugh (I certainly catch those of his friends) because he is all right, and is quickly executing ever more skilful tricks.

Dank-smelling water rushes down the weir, ripples closely packed like someone's crinkly grey hair in old age, stretching across the river between two arms which guide water into the weir itself. Fishermen line the banks, shallow below and for some way towards the middle. A man wields his rod from the saddle of a pushbike parked in a foot of water, and another tries his luck from a wooden kitchen chair. They make themselves at home by Beeston Lock, and catch those fish which are deceived into thinking that all will be well after the hurly-burly of the weir.

A notice nailed to a tree says NO NIGHT FISHING, meaning I suppose that a bailiff can't be paid to look for you in darkness and claim his fee. A red day-flying cinnabar moth flutters over the fullpacked heads of healthy wheat. Summer vegetation is still luxuriant, the river bank lined with thick jungle. Crows caw over Clifton Grove, where striated cliffs show between dark trees in streaks of orange. Nothing disturbs my plain walk through the greensward except a notice announcing that the land belongs to Nottingham University, which means I am getting closer to the city. Far away to the left are chimneys, containers, factories, storehouses and, of course, the clock tower of the university itself.

When the area was open fields I used to come here with my sisters and brothers, five of us aged from ten down to three, carrying sandwiches and a bottle of water. We played by a dredger, swinging on chains that hung over the water. The return walk was six miles, so that by the time we got home we were almost carrying each other.

The ever-present river is an easy mark of navigation. You can't go wrong. The Clifton roadbridge funnels traffic around the city, but the wheatfields continue. Poppies and saxifrage line the riverbank,

126

a secret route into town. Dressed in camouflage jacket and trousers, one could avoid roadblocks and be unobserved, hardly visible in that subtle finger of green crooked towards the heart of the city.

Wilford across the river is where Henry Kirke White lived, and maundered over fields writing reams of unreadable poetry. Born in 1785 (it's his bicentenary year, but no one has noticed), he was the son of a Nottingham butcher, and helped his father for a time. After a stint as a stocking weaver he worked for an attorney. Considered a promising poet by Robert Southey among others, cash was raised to send him to Cambridge, a fatal act of benevolence, because he worked too hard and died of consumption at twenty-one. He was best known in his time for the hymn 'Much in sorrow, oft in woe' and his chief poem was called 'The Christiad'.

Fairham Brook, which runs into the river south of Wilford, was once surrounded by meadows, but is now lost between houses. My parents took us on picnics there, a mile from the Narrow Marsh district in town where we lived. A white gate opened off the lane, and a footbridge led over the stream, the path continuing to Clifton Grove.

At Trentside Farm I swing the waterbottle over my mouth for a drink, and the driver of a passing tractor calls: 'Five star brandy, then?'

I offer some, but he thinks it's water, and laughs a refusal. The Castle is to the left, and Wilford power station straight ahead – where a coalmine used to be. By the river there's so much greenery it feels as if I'm still in the country, but the footpath ends abruptly and leads on to a shaded walk by the roadside. We used to call Wilford Bridge 'Ha'penny Bridge', because it cost that much (or that little) to get over. The difference between the Meadows area packed with houses and Wilford village among fields on the other side was total. It was worth the ha'penny to walk into paradise. Before 1870 people crossed by a ferry, and in 1784 the overloaded boat capsized, drowning six passengers on their way home from market.

The embankment enters the city, skirting a park laid out around the War Memorial in the twenties. By four o'clock I'm on the main

Trent Bridge, built in 1871. A bridge has existed here since Saxon times, and the present span replaced a stone structure around which there were several skirmishes during the Civil War between the King's troops and Cromwell's Roundheads.

The day's stint is ended, but I walk another mile or so to a friend's house on the edge of West Bridgford, where my car is parked, making a day's plod of nearly thirteen miles.

Lodgings are scarce this evening. I drive from one colourfully lit hostelry to another. By the reception desk, only cursorily attended, I look through to the crowded bar. None can offer a bed: 'Full to the gills!' one frenetic but happy manager tells me. Such has been my preoccupation with the day's walk that I had forgotten the Test Match was on.

Nine-tenths cloud, ten o'clock, muggy. I avoid the Trent as it flows through the city, and set off from Carlton, having stayed the night at my brother's. The met office predicts showers, so I expect to play cat-and-mouse with the weather much of the day.

The familiar smell of coal smoke lingers in the streets, even in summer, as well as the strong odour of burning vegetation from back gardens. Beyond one hedge, plate-headed chrysanthemums of various colours are taller even than the cloth-capped gardener who wields large scissors nearby, as if to decide which flowers he will cut for a funeral. Perhaps he's going to see a girlfriend. More likely – by the look of him – he's been married forty years, and wakes his wife with a fine bloom every morning, a habit he acquired since his redundancy (or retirement) from the railway five years ago. When available, he lays a chrysanthemum on her breakfast tray, as an offering for a peaceful day.

The sight of so many yellow, pink, carmine and orange flowertops produces semi-hallucinations as I play roulette with the traffic on crossing the dual carriageway, symptoms of drink no doubt from the night before. I suppose such gaudy flowerheads suggested the punk style to imaginative youngsters, hairdos created after a copycat glance over a garden fence.

128

Under a railway bridge, and back on to a street, my brother's instructions for finding the footpath to Stoke Bardolph vanish in the wind. The brain can't take them in, and neither is the map much good in such terrain, though I finally find a lane to the river which covers the same mileage.

Chipmunk trainers, probably doing circuits and bumps with a cadet on board, fly out of Newton a couple of miles across the river. They nibble through low cloud, and the time warp takes me back to being fifteen when I queued for a trip outside the flight office and, no nonsense about insurance in those days, a Polish pilot got ten of us into a De Havilland Dominie biplane, and winged us over the river to have a look at Nottingham. My view of the world changed. Two engines kept us going at a hundred miles an hour, and from being an ant I had become a bird – though only for twenty minutes. Humanity was a thousand feet below, and I was privileged in being detached from all those who could not be where I was. The ground plan of the factory I worked at was flat like a target map, and from that moment I decided not to go back into it for any longer than necessary, though two years elapsed before the pledge was made good.

Once more an ant, I walk towards Stoke Bardolph. Lines of pylons beyond the river are faint in the morning light. A vast sewage establishment discreetly shelters behind a belt of trees. The warm and muggy weather doesn't do much for the stench – subtle though it is – but a lovely smell of roses greets me as water meadows by the river come into view. A line of elegant lamp posts in the yard of Lowes Farm are painted yellow and green and white. The Ferry Boat Inn is of course closed, and there isn't a ferry any more. A drain, presumably from the aforementioned sewage farm, throws a white stain several hundred yards down the river, on which two orange-jacketed men in a kayak paddle merrily. The atmosphere sizzles as I walk under a line of pylons.

The river is so placid I'm tempted to hire a canoe and make my arms work instead of my legs, except that at many places the banks would be too high to see over. The weightiest items in my pack are a jumbo flask of tea and an army waterbottle, otherwise things are

Riverfront – Newark

in the pockets of my walking jacket or, such as compass and
binoculars, hang around my neck. Staying overnight in bed-and-
breakfast places allows me to travel light.

   A sixty-year-old woman wearing a spotted frock, with a large
black dog for company, sits on a campstool. By her in the water rests
a catchnet, and she holds a long rod, and at the end of her line a
float bobs in the current. This is Anglers' Valley, ever-shallow though
it is, because there's hardly a time when you don't see someone
fishing. I've never fished, but the sport seems quiet, not apparently
competitive, and obviously soothing, and draws more people, I hear,
than football matches at the weekend.

   Either the woman's husband has gone for a pint (too early, or I
would be in the same bar) or it is her habit and pleasure to angle
alone. She is a widow and comes fishing because she used to do it
with her husband. Or maybe she has never been married and did it
with her father, or brother. Or she has done it all her life with none
of them. So why is she fishing on the Trent at eleven o'clock on a
midweek in July and looking so obviously pleased with herself? She
wishes me good morning, with a smile.

   Before Burton Joyce – over a stile and back on to the footpath –
a line of poplars leads to the village. Two crows and a gull lift from
the shore. Sheep sleep on the opposite bank, framed by the sharp
outline of Shelford church tower. From Malkin Hill I got my first view
of the river after cycling up from Radcliffe.

   The flat land between Shelford and the river is called The Hams,
and on this side Burton Meadows. A regular breeze makes it cool
going, which is good. There's still the ubiquitous growl of Chipmunk
trainers from Newton, and through binoculars I see the orange
windsock fully outblown. The river turns gunmetal blue, and I hope
it won't rain. Huge purple thistle flowers bordering the path shine
as if they have a light inside.

   A few walls and barns of Shelford Manor are visible between the
trees. The Royalists had it through much of the Civil War. Their main
force was at Newark, fifteen miles away, while Nottingham was in
the hands of Colonel Hutchinson and the Parliamentarians. The

Shelford garrison, by controlling the Trent valley, was a thorn in Nottingham's side. The Royalists also held Belvoir Castle, eleven miles south-east, and active patrols from the two places seriously interfered with Nottingham's communications. When Shelford was attacked, snipers who defended the church tower were soon smoked out. One was a woman corporal, whose fate is not known. Another prisoner was a youth who had recently switched allegiance, but his life was spared after he revealed the weak part in the Royalists' defences.

The Manor was fortified, and stood by the river about a mile away. Its garrison of two hundred men put up a resistance which so maddened the attackers that no quarter was given when the place surrendered. A hundred and forty Royalists were slaughtered, and Colonel Stanhope, their commander, was stripped for dead and thrown on to a dungheap. The house went up in flames, and only forty of the defenders were alive when the butchery stopped. Most were Roman Catholics, which was one of the reasons why they were treated without pity. After the Restoration Colonel Hutchinson was to die a miserable death at Deal Castle in Kent.

A pretty horsewoman gives me a smile as she canters by, which is gladly returned, the mutual recognition of those who are not using petrol as they move from place to place. The bridle path through summery wheatfields is pleasant indeed, and there's more of a sparkle to the widening river as it laps at wooded banks and ripples on its way to the sea. The track turns east, and at midday I go under Gunthorpe Bridge to a riverside village of pubs, shops, cottages and bungalows. There's also a restaurant and a post office. All facilities, as the guidebooks say.

I sit over a cup of coffee (coffee? More like hot water in which an acorn's been dipped, and then only briefly. English tea and coffee are so miserably nondescript that if you don't take sugar you might as well order hot water. The biggest profit loss must be in the sweetening).

The name of Lowdham springs off the map, a village two miles away, probably known for little more these days than its 'HM Youth

Custody Centre'. But in the early nineteenth century a dark and satanic mill stood there. The story is told by Robert Blincoe, an orphan at the St Pancras workhouse where, he said, he was not badly treated. In August 1799 he was one of eighty children who were tricked into volunteering to be apprenticed to a firm of cotton spinners at Lowdham Mill. On setting out from London each child was provided with two suits of clothes, a new handkerchief, a shilling, and a large piece of gingerbread. Two wagons with grated doors took them on their journey, and when they clambered down four days later the people of Lowdham could only say: 'God help the poor wretches'.

Their diet was miserable and insufficient, and they were driven to their benches at five-thirty each morning by a man with a horsewhip. They worked fourteen and sometimes sixteen hours a day, and were savagely beaten if they showed signs of slacking. Robert Blincoe ran away, but was caught by a Methodist tailor, who took him back to the mill singing hymns as he went – to claim his reward of five shillings.

Local magistrates who heard complaints about the apprentices' treatment ordered a new house to be built, and better food provided. Conditions improved. They were given knives, forks and spoons, and issued with bedding. Every Sunday they went to church wearing new suits, and were escorted once a year to the Goose Fair at Nottingham, with sixpence to spend. Blincoe considers that they were, finally, humanely treated, but unfortunately Lowdham Mill closed and the children were transferred to one at Tideswell in Derbyshire. There they were so barbarously done by that they died by the dozen, and no one could come to their aid because the mill owner himself happened to be a magistrate – and a rich man. He distributed the bodies of his victims to different cemeteries in an effort to conceal the numerous deaths.

In general apprentices were reasonably well treated, but it often happened that when they went on to the labour market at twenty-one years of age they couldn't find work because a man's wage was due to them. Times have changed from the worst of the bad old days.

Human life is more valuable, at least in certain pockets of the world where it isn't too thick on the ground, and where there are sufficient riches underneath and on its surface.

A notice says: 'Dangerous Waters. Do Not Swim'. Insidious and sly, the old river has always been known for untrustworthiness. Lights on red at Gunthorpe Lock mean that you wait your turn to go downstream. White water foams over the weir, and if you speed over that you're as good as dead – or as drowned as a rat. A footbridge crosses, and thus spans the river.

The valley becomes picturesque in the Victorian guidebook sense, heavily wooded hills rising to 250 feet on the opposite bank, making as pretty a bit of river as anywhere in England.

A man who I think is a farmhand asks in a friendly fashion as he walks by: 'Where are *you* going, then?'

'Me?' I answer. 'I'm walking the Trent – as far as Gainsborough.'

'Bloody good luck to you, mate,' he says merrily.

Not rowing it, sailing it, paddling it or steaming down it under coal, but tramping the turf in the old style to keep an eye on its antics. I turn, and see that he is looking at me as if I'm on my first day out of Broadmoor. Well, who knows?

A footpath on the other side winds among the trees, and the warbling of doves makes my tramp entirely bucolic. Cows graze and water at the riverbank near Glebe Farm. Cattle aren't shy, like sheep. You can walk close. A line of stricken elms near Hoveringham are mourned by cries of the gulls. A green and black barge called the *Béhomoth* comes up river. There's a brief kiss of the sun, and no sign of a ferry at Hoveringham, but I get a cool double fruit juice at the bar of the Old Elm Tree Inn, which looks such a good place to have lunch that I'm almost sorry to be carrying my own.

A hawthorn tree has a pillow underneath, and I wonder how it got there. There is no one to come and put their head down, and it doesn't look clean enough for my own. Eating lunch by the track, I feel a spray of rain, hoping it won't come to much, though in fifteen minutes I'm on my way in case it does.

Gravel excavations over the embankment have left extensive water

Cow Meadows

areas: 'Danger. Deep Water and Quick Sands. Keep Out. The Company disclaims all liability for accident or injury to unauthorised persons entering these premises.' Then come wheatfields and a quiet part of the river far from any motorable lane.

Syerston aerodrome across the river was a bomber base during the war. I flew in the tail gunner's turret of a Lancaster, to as far from Nottingham as I was to get till a troopship took me to Malaya. I flew in Douglas Dakotas, and did circuits-and-bumps in Hamilcar gliders, and always the navigationally secure Trent was the first landmark manifest after lifting from the end of the runway. The prevailing westerly wind was in favour of that direction, and those who lived on that side of the river during the war must have heard bombers taking off night after night. All you get nowadays is the buzzing of Chipmunks from Newton.

At one annual camp, looking forward to many cadged rides, I fell ill, and didn't come out of the sick quarters till it was time to go home. What was wrong I never knew. I didn't ask, and nobody told me. Perhaps they didn't know, either, though I think it was either the flu, or exhaustion, because I had certainly been done-for on staggering in to see the MO. I slept for several days, and when I came to there was a quart of cold milk by my bed which I drank straight off. I was still groggy when I got back to Nottingham, but clocked in at the factory on Monday morning nevertheless. I had never been in any hospital before, nor was I to be again until my next incarceration, which was for far longer, and also in an RAF hospital.

I float so intensely among such memories during my walk that they feel like active reality that I have stepped back into and can only get out of with an effort. I feel that the more memories you have the deeper you can dive down into yourself. The danger is that you'll get stuck in the mud or weeds, unable to come up, strike air, and go on living to create more memories. As soon as you stop churning out things to remember, you're dead.

So I walk. Thistles line one side of the track, facing ranks of Queen Anne's lace. Both plants are tall, and threaten each other as if about to join battle. A red admiral butterfly flits from side to side like a

136

plenipotentiary trying to make peace. I stroll through, wondering if it will succeed, noticing a score of cows on the opposite bank whose skins are the colour of light saddlebag leather.

A power station marked on the adjoining map sheet has cooling towers like the jars which hid Ali Baba in the cave of the forty thieves. I won't get there for a while. At Bleasby an RAF air sea rescue pinnace is moored outside the Star and Garter. I would have expected no less, though it does seem a long way from its base of operations. A small caravan bears a notice indicating that it sells 'BAIT AND . . .' What the rest is I shall never know. Across the river where the ferry used to be stands a green hut which may have been used by the ferryman. Maybe someone still lives there, but it's not Mr Charon.

Two small motorboats come upriver. A barge goes down, and another comes up. The rule of the waterway, busy at this point, is continental in that you travel on the right. I dodge into the Star and Garter for another double fruit juice – a large building where you can also get accommodation. The caravan parks do good trade in high summer.

The river sweeps around an island called The Nabs, and another weir has the usual lock to go with it. Rain sprinkles but, please God, doesn't open up. Wooded hills border the other side of the river, while on my side there are wheatfields. Underfoot is river gravel, red loam and alluvium.

At Hazelford it says: 'All persons traversing this weir in a canoe or other craft do so entirely at their own risk. The Board accept no liability for any damage to property or persons arising from this practice.' Which makes it sound rather immoral, though I observe a barge waiting to have a go, like a soldier outside a knocking shop in Benghazi.

A footbridge crosses the weir, and therefore the river, but the iron gate is locked and another intimidating notice prohibits any traverse. Why pedestrians aren't allowed to use them, now that ferries no longer operate, is hard to say. Perhaps the British Waterways Board fear that one or two may chuck themselves from the catwalk into

137

the hypnotising foam – another practice which would (rightly) be frowned upon. It may not be economical to maintain ferries (or maybe it would, who knows?), but it would be a great advantage to hikers and others to be able to cross the river at such points.

The weir is impressive. A certain amount of water comes down, but another part is channelled at an angle of ninety degrees, both falls built in a series of seven steps, down which water forcefully tumbles.

An RAF Hawker Siddeley Argosy passes over – four-engined, twin-boomed, twin-tailed – looking for a lost pinnace perhaps, though it continues south-east, as if assuming that the crew has already reached the fleshpots of Nottingham.

Another map sheet is called for, and while the grass is equally thick and high the trail becomes less marked, certainly not worn to the mud as heretofore, though one or two anglers statuesquely pose at the bank, often not easy to see in their green clothing. One of them looks up surprised because he thinks I'm talking to myself, not seeing the small technological tape-recorder notebook in my hand.

Across the river is Ladies Piece, a pretty enough name, but in the wood behind is Red Gutter, a sunken road descending from the hill. The village of East Stoke over the brow gave its name to the battle of 16 June 1487, a fight which ended the Wars of the Roses, the bloodiest and most futile conflict fought on English soil.

An Oxford priest on the Yorkist side had schooled a bright-eyed boy of ten, Lambert Simnel, son of an Oxford tradesman, as pretender to the throne of Henry VII. It's hard to imagine a more forlorn (not to say stupid) hope, looking back on it, but among the five thousand men of the rebel forces were two thousand German mercenaries commanded by Martin Swartz. This time they chose the wrong employer, because none survived the battle. Nor did a thousand ferocious half-naked Irishmen who also took up the cause of the rebels.

The King marched out of Nottingham to defend his crown, and at the end of the day seven thousand corpses lay in and around the Red Gutter and on Dead Man's Field. The boy pretender was taken

138

alive and, permitted to work as a scullion in the King's household, eventually rose to the position of Royal Falconer.

Near Stoke vicarage is a spring whose water never fails or freezes. Legend says that such a phenomenon was promised by a wounded soldier to a country man who gave him a drink from it.

When I went over the battlefield above the Red Gutter a falling rain soddened the ground, and miles of open country were visible from the slight rise. To my left, a lone biker was bombing up the Fosse Way, twin headlamps winking in the dusk, rain pouring down. A few birds sang, but the clamour of battle seemed to drown them, as men quarrelled and bolstered themselves, and prepared for the fight. It was a depressing place.

I set out with a friend for Newark when I was sixteen, to bike the twenty miles from Nottingham and back. We battled full of energy up the Fosse Way in an adverse wind, intent on reaching our destination. But at Stoke we became silent, and discouraged without knowing why. Hardly discussing the matter, we turned round, and immediately felt more cheerful.

The weather makes for eeriness. Later, when it was fine and warm, I went down to the river, where the old ferry crossing used to be. All that's left is a bank spectacularly rich in white convolvulus, rose bay, dying nettles, and foxgloves on their last legs. Where the pub had gone I couldn't say, though to the left of the track a building was falling into decrepitude.

I found the Red Gutter by pacing its location out from the map, a nondescript part of the wood with no special features except a slight declivity. The trees grow rich, but then they always do, whether it's blood or rain that feeds them. It's the soil that counts.

The Pretender's beaten troops almost got to the flat and open land in their effort to escape the butchering ferocity of Henry's soldiers. Maybe a few made it to the river. 16 June 1987 will be the 500th anniversary of the battle, memorable if only for the odds against the success of the rebels, though I guess there will be no one to mourn the slain as at Bosworth Field.

A jet of water irrigates a field, rocketing in a straight line. The

The Trent at Nottingham

mechanism is subjected to the variation of the wind, and the wind, being erratic, changes suddenly and allows it to send an incredible trajectory of water in a totally different direction. A strong south-wester backs and tacks, changing the path of the water every few seconds.

The river is canalised at Fiskerton, site of the ferry crossing which Martin Swartz and his Germans tried to reach after the Stoke carnage. The first pub in the village is the Bromley Arms, and I am encouraged at turning the door handle to find the place open. I reach the bar, but the publican comes in and tells me the place is closed. I'm nine minutes late. Another double something or other would have been welcome.

There are two Chipmunks in the sky now, doing formation flying. Are they following me? A pretty barge called the *Singing Swan* comes upriver. I would rather be on a barge than walking, especially during the hours when the pubs are so definitely shut. On a barge, I ruminate, you can tow a crate of beer in the water, or stash a few bottles in a cabin out of the sun.

Attractive houses line the riverfront at Fiskerton-cum-Morton. Fishing is under the auspices of the Nottingham Piscatorial Society, meaning it is very private. A gleaming new seat bench on the footpath allows me to admire the view in comfort. The beautifully carpentered seat is fixed on to a concrete base, and a brass plaque says: 'In memory of TJ Jim Watson, a friend of the NPS 1985'. I lounge back and finish the tea in my flask. Thank you, Jim.

Three miles north lies the cathedral at Southwell, an elegant building surrounded by the neatest town in Nottinghamshire. I went there during the war, on a bus which called at every village along the river, and I marked each of them off on my first black-and-white one-inch Ordnance map, by then on sale in the shops. Near Southwell, Brackenhurst Hall was the home of Field Marshal Lord Allenby, liberator of Palestine from the Turks in the First World War, a man who has many streets named after him in Israel.

The river wiggles towards Staythorpe power station, the footpath hardly marked but the way obvious. The opposite bank shows park-like grounds about Stoke Hall, a mid-sixteenth-century edifice standing back from the river among elm, beech and chestnut trees. I can see the façade and many chimneys of the Hall, with a kind of chapel tower above the stables. The nearby Wharf Farm, on the Fosse Way, is only three miles from Newark in a straight line, but by following the contrary river I shall have to do over five.

A notice opposite says that mooring and picnicking are prohibited, by order of the farm owners. Maybe, and quite rightly, they are afraid of a boatload of gay young things spreading corks and biscuit crumbs over the immaculate greensward; or of a high-speed omnibus whose driver, tired from zooming up the Fosse Way, tips his football special out for a puke-up and fist fight on the Trent's quiet banks. I don't blame them. The stretch is peaceful and clean, though traffic noise can be heard from the road.

On the most isolated part of the walk there are no fishermen or anyone else out for the pleasure of a stroll. Power transmission lines cross the river, and then I pass two more water-dragons turning the land into a quagmire rather than irrigating it.

A man sits fishing near the power station while his wife knits. For three miles I've been waiting for the river to change direction on this most *schleppy* part of the walk. Near the Farndon Sailing Club, beyond the marvellous smell of a mown field, is a lorry graveyard. How they got there is anybody's guess. There are no lanes, but maybe they were punted into place before the ferry closed down. Jet fighters swoop. The power station is close, but never close enough. At three o'clock Farndon Harbour is across the river. A white launch bristles with aerials and flies the Red Duster. That's the boat I would like – a superb river-roamer, safe from spiteful sea or playful tide.

Two swans make aggressive gestures, but I don't deviate or alter my plodding rate. After beating about a bush the one nearest the bank displays a full wingspread and a forward thrusting neck, as if braced for a short-tempered take-off. Am I supposed to admire its handsome appearance? Reflected in the water, it seems there are two, and that the other will get me if the first fails.

I envisage my line of retreat – away from the water: I run, but am forced to turn and face the rage of my pursuer. With stout boots and a jack-knife it'll be a close-run encounter. Should have carried a walking stick (or even a knobkerrie) but they realise I have no wish to strangle their cygnets, and fold the wings back, as if they are then going to disappear into a hangar under the water. The ripples subside, and all is peace again.

Poppies, white daisies and purple thistles make a medley of colour along the path. The massive power station buildings at Staythorpe stretch along the river like the Houses of Parliament – the Commons of Power – a magnificent terrace similar to that on the Thames, though the buildings don't shelter people who talk, but house machines that provide energy. A stepping stone crosses the river via the weir, which tempts me, but they're a little too far apart, and the water rushes over the stones that have too much moss to allow a sure footing.

The sound of turbines and generators drowns the gnatwhine of a low flying jet. I don't linger at this Battersea-on-Trent, but follow the path towards Averham. The trouble is I can't find the place where it goes under (or over?) the railway. After some reconnoitring I notice that the line crosses the Trent, and that a footway goes alongside towards Newark. The only obstacle to its use is a notice (another bloody notice!) saying: 'Right of Way Act, 1932. This footpath is private property and is for the use of Central Electricity Generating Board employees only. Trespassers are forbidden by order. Speed limit 10 mph.'

Putting a spanner behind my ear, as it were, lighting a Woodbine, setting my workman's cap at a jaunty angle, and assuming for the moment a Nelsonic illiteracy, I decide that this is to be my way onward. The track is too narrow for cars but sufficient for cycles and mopeds, though I expect the local ton-up boys play mayhem on it now and again.

Walking between the bifurcations of the Trent, I'm fenced off from the railway embankment to my left, and to the right from the private property of extensive meadows. According to the map the paved track will take me to the station in Newark, straight for at least a mile, though I can't see all the way because of a humpbacked bridge over the Old Trent Dyke, which must play hell with the bikers during their two-stroke rodeos.

The paving isn't so kind on my feet as the riverside turf, and because of a sore heel I name my thoroughfare Wincing Lane. The railway veers, and I come to one of those half-concealed rubbish dumps which are found on the outskirts of every town. To enumerate the contents of the squalid heap would call forth a catalogue of human woes, and I refrain because the day is now warm and sunny.

The first houses appear, and blue plastic bags hang in the hedgerows where there had formerly been flowers. Such half-secret ways into every town are familiar to the local getaway artists. Bill Posters, ever in danger of being prosecuted, has them all marked on his Nottinghamshire operations map.

Mountains of rusting cars form a bizarre topography in a breaker's yard, and an intense smell of honeysuckle comes from a cottage garden. Newark church spire and the ruins of the Castle are across a caravan park, just over the old river itself. A notice in the back window of a van says: 'Vampires are a pain in the neck'. Maybe the inhabitants of Newark felt the same about the Roundheads and Scots who besieged them in 1645, and possibly also about the Royalists who were quartered there. The siege ended quite humanely, but then came the plague, which was an even bigger pain in the neck.

The cattle market is empty as, I assume, is the Castle opposite. At the main road I look for a sign pointing to the station. From the map I know where it ought to be, and yet it seems not to be in the ruinous district which is to my left. But it is. The road leading there is grass grown, as if the last vehicles to rumble that way were the supply wagons of King Charles I.

The building has a British Rail logo of the admass age totally out of character with the decrepitude of darkening bricks. The ramshackle buildings seem about to fall down, as if a bomber boy had passed that way and only half his explosive charge went off. There is neither ticket office, waiting room nor buffet. A couple of disconsolate backpackers sit on the floor of the platform, and a few

144

Fishermen

people look into space as if they would rather be somewhere else. A porter or guard doesn't want any truck with possible passengers in case one of them – me – should have the cheek to ask him the time of the next train to Nottingham. Someone else tells me, though not too willingly either. Ten minutes later the train comes, and in half an hour takes me in fourteen straight miles what had needed nineteen to do along the river.

I spend the night at Lowes Farm, Stoke Bardolph (bed and breakfast £8) where I left my car to serve as a mobile base. The window of my attic room looks across the road and over the river. At five-thirty in the morning visibility is about three hundred yards, and I almost expect to see the Ark go by under the deluge. A field of Jersey cows bellow in alarm at flashes of lightning that even the Trent power stations can't match, at least not so spectacularly.

Before getting back into bed I see fishermen walking along both banks, in spite of explosions and the downpour. They move over meadows and against a background of woods, as if to cut off the bend of the river, carrying bags and appurtenances sticking up like army kit. In their olive and green drab they look like a First World War patrol, wire running along this side of the river giving the scene verisimilitude.

At the banquet of a breakfast are two fishermen who have not gone out. The rain washes energetically down. They are friends, and come every year from Lancashire. The talkative bald-headed one says he used to go to the Fens, but with so much conservation going on down there, utilisation of water, rearrangement of dykes etcetera, it is no longer any good. The Trent, a fine fishing river, is better value. The two men seem well suited because the other, who has a good head of dark hair, says not a word.

The Castle Barge moored on the Trent at Newark advertises Good Ale and Hearty Food. You can eat on deck, on the wharf, or go below and sup products of North Country Breweries at the long bar. The vessel is coloured yellow, terracotta, marine blue, and has a

146

spectacular superstructure of red, green, black and brown, with ample technicolour bunting and an incredibly tall mast, the whole set against a background of warehouses across the river. They like colour in Newark.

From the bus station I go on over the bridge and begin the day's walk to Dunham. A footpath passes the usual derelict buildings, a mountain of smashed and besmirched motor corpses between trees on the opposite bank. The brewery trade in Newark began in 1776, the same year as the American Declaration of Independence, started perhaps on the melancholic assumption that if you can't win 'em, get drunk.

Redbricked ruins have a sadder aspect than other kinds, buildings not picturesquely neglected, but looking rather as if someone tried to light a fire inside them and failed. Half a bridge, half a house, a few fishermen engrossed in silent confrontation with the fishes, but glancing back you see only unoccupied factories and abandoned breweries. (Driving out of town a few days later, the fronts of some buildings gave the impression of being in use. Their façades were clean and intact, and suggested active prosperity, though I wondered whether they weren't Potemkin structures (or Thatcher Buildings), part of a scheme as in much of the rest of England to put a jaunty face on the worst excesses of the decline.)

A footbridge leads to the east bank and under a railway bridge. A huge sewage farm in full production suggests that such places will be working to the last, and the storage towers of a sugarbeet factory across the river indicate that dentists will have no difficulty finding work to the edge of doom, either. The only other signs of civilisation are numbered dabs of concrete, as posts for fishing licences.

Each individual sprig of tall reed grass ahead has heavy globules of sparkling water which shake with fervour at the prospect of leaping on to me when I get close. There's nothing to do but brush past, so that my trousers and legs are soon saturated. Boots said to be proof against all liquid let cold water through to the skin and weigh as heavy as lead.

The Great North Road crosses the river, and a man with a book of permits in his hand asks if I'm going fishing. Perhaps he senses a sale.

'No,' I answer. 'I'm on a walking trip.'

'Pub's a mile up the road, then,' he quips.

They're a cheery lot in Nottinghamshire, I tell myself, thanking him for the information and plodding on over the soggy ground. He only told me about the pub because he knows it'll be closed. The uncertain weather does not make for a good mood.

The grass beyond the bridge, chewed short by sheep and cattle, is a great improvement. All I need is for the sun to come out and dry my boots and trousers, though you can't have everything. I am on Winthorpe Rack (or Reach) not far from the village of the same name. An aviation museum at the nearby airfield costs a pound to get into. The large hut of exhibits – posters, maps, radio equipment and sundry technical gear from the interiors of aircraft (they must have been through the famous Lawrence Corner shop in London) – are badly illuminated. In the outside compound are wrecks and relics of planes. There's a Hastings, a Percival Proctor, an Avro Shackleton, a Gloster Meteor, a Varsity Trainer, a Heron (no engines), various helicopters, and an Avro Vulcan which must have been acquired after the Falklands War – all true grist for the aero-buff's mill. The only item to give a flicker of nostalgia is the sort of black and white chequerboard 'caravan' I worked in at Langar.

Traffic is audible from the Great North Road, whose dual carriageway follows the river for some miles beyond Winthorpe Lake and Holme Village. A paved lane before Cromwell lock goes parallel to part of the bank known as The Oven, though I can't think why on such a damp summer's day.

Cromwell weir is a steely, powerful fall of water, where sun and blue sky at midday inspire me to have lunch. The curving Trent is regimented as far as fishermen are concerned, because every ten or fifteen yards, and for some miles by wheatfields and posses of cows, a white post bearing a number is staked in the ground.

Beyond gorgeously headed purple thistles, acres of golden maize wave in the wind, a foil to the blue and rippling waterway. Small

148

monoplanes do stunts between the clouds, a comforting sound so much part of the countryside that I would miss it if it stopped.

All the pretty villages seem to be on the other bank, where I imagine that one can get afternoon tea at many of the cottages, with hot scones and bramble jelly and the tastiest of non-teabag Indian tea. Close by Carlton church is a windmill.

Consciousness while walking creates a different kind of prison to one with walls. The prison becomes one of space, whose agreeable pictures confine by their sameness because they change so slowly, a treadmill with apparently unchanging scenery. Wanting to get away from the eternal presence of the river, I begin a diversion to escape a zone of gravel diggings and machinery which line the bank ahead. In any case, there is no public footpath for a mile or so, and I am nothing (today) if not law-abiding.

The leafy lane running east towards Besthorpe has many pools of water. Traffic noise on the A1 highway dims, and after a kilometre I turn NNW along an equally soddened trackway. Spot heights on the map, of seven and nine metres, testify to the flatness of the land. Stretches of water on either side of the path have sides too straight to be natural. Gravel pits in this area are what opencast coalmining is further west. The water that remains is good for birds, if nothing else.

The path bifurcates, then trifurcates, and from an embankment I see huge machines robbing the fields of their green blanket. Hedges and the landmarks of ditches have disappeared. Ruts made by earth removers are so deep that I stumble into them and have to clamber out. I regret not having a 1:25,000 scale map showing more detail, but I deduce that there's a substantial stream to get over called The Fleet, which must be located before I can resume the riverside track. The no man's land is so convoluted and ripped about that even the direction to the river is lost.

Along the edge of a field there is much grinding and drumming of machinery, of pumps heaving water into a drainage ditch. Other pipes proliferate, but I see no sign of people. Trespassing is the least of my worries, though I now regret that I didn't stay by the river

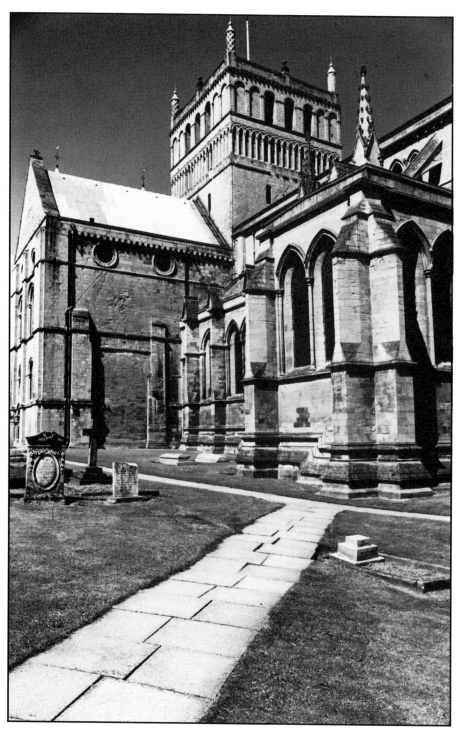

Southwell Minster

and go through the gravel working machinery, which would have been easy compared to this.

A solid hedge is reinforced by a fence and a ditch. I must get over and, as often in such cases, throw my pack on to the other side so that, come what may, I must go after it.

The ditch seems reasonably dry, but the fence is unstable. Strands of barbed wire cunningly lace the parapet, and I don't want to rip my jacket or trousers. My forlorn pack beckons from the other side like a long-lost friend, and I throw my binoculars across to keep it company until such time as we will become one happy unit again. To settle matters I skim the map over as well.

I find footholds, and slowly level myself to the ridge-like summit of what seems more like a fortification than a field boundary. It wobbles under my feet, however, and I am tempted to jump, but branches and wire are like a greedy hedgehog between me and the ground. As if admiring the view I balance, above all keeping cool, though even from here I can't make out the course of the river. Instead of a dramatic header on to the grass I seek footholds half-way down.

I jump, and the ditch is behind me, in which water flows vigorously under its covering of reedgrass bent by the wind. The commonest navigational error is to think you are further than you are but, looking at the map, I know my approximate position, and roughly where the river lies. I steer a compass course, there being no trace of a footpath across Smithy Marsh, and instinct as much as anything brings me to a bridge over The Fleet – a positive mark on the map. Back at the Trent, I assume that all gravel diggings are left behind.

Turning a bend, there's another city of machinery along the bank: tin huts, trackways, and various structures whose purpose is to bash stones and sort pebbles, hemmed in by enormous pyramids of clean gravel. Still, the area seems to offer an easy way through, compared to my recent scramble over the assault course. Children are not allowed to wander on their own, a notice says, in an attempt to safeguard them from disappearing without trace in this jumble of

151

giant-sized toys. Tall reservoirs, with narrow aqueducts running in all directions and from all heights cross my path, but I duck under one after another and get on my way. The Republic of Gravellonia is left behind.

Normal walking resumes over grass so lush I think it no wonder that cows who feed on it grow to such sleekness. The river meanders towards pylons, but it would be a mistake to think that the walk is spoiled by quarries and power stations, because the land is meadow-like and open, and satisfies every craving for isolation.

Four miles beyond the other side of the river lies Harby, near the Lincolnshire border, where Eleanor of Castile, wife of Edward I, died in 1290. 'I loved her tenderly in her lifetime,' the King said, 'and I do not cease to love her now she is dead.' Full of sorrow, he took her body to Lincoln to be embalmed, then carted it by slow stages to Westminster Abbey, resting places on the way marked by 'Eleanor Crosses'. The last stop was at Charing, which became Charing Cross.

Nottinghamshire place names often have different meanings for me, because by looking at the map I sometimes imagine them as characters in novels, building people from the ground up, as it were. Pearl Harby is one such person, as is Ernest Cotgrave the storyteller, and the old soldier Oxton in *The Widower's Son*. A name on a topographical map marks a person with a face and a past that might not have come to mind in any other way. Such labels often turn into names that fit, though I suppose one can also ask: What's in a name?

Beyond Marnham power station the grass is springy and dry, and I sit down on it to have tea and biscuits. From feeling suddenly done-for, energy rushes back, and the realisation that it is caused by food is a reminder that one's consciousness is capable of neglecting the needs of the body if you don't watch it. It's useful to remember that eating is a good alternative to walking, and that you must stoke up little but often.

Fledborough church across the river has a Danish neatness about it. From 1721 to 1753 it was used to administer speedy wedlock as at Gretna Green. In 1820 Dr Thomas Arnold, the headmaster of Rugby School, was married there.

152

I regret not having a shotgun, because numerous rabbits skim from my path. Those with cunning dive for cover with alacrity, while the stupid ones can't decide when to get out of the way, and keep on running in full view. Which type would make the more delicious feast is hard to say. A wooded cliff to the right must be full of burrows.

Traffic is held up to pay a toll of fifteen pence to cross the river near Dunham. The last time I went over the bridge was on a bike in April 1944. The previous day I had cycled with a friend from Nottingham to Wainfleet, south of Skegness. We spent the night in a concrete pillbox on the beach and, with a driftwood fire at the entrance, made ourselves as comfortable as the bitter Easter weather would allow. Next morning we cycled to Skegness, ate some beans on toast, and set off for Nottingham.

We cycled through Horncastle and over the Lincolnshire Wolds, and because it was Sunday – and wartime – we could get nothing to eat. At Dunham, sixty miles from our pillbox on the beach, we were done-in and hungry, wet to the bone from the rain. Every door was closed against us. At dusk we reached Tuxford, seven more miles, which seemed as long as all the other miles put together. But at least we were inside the Nottinghamshire boundary, and saw a house offering bed and breakfast. The woman fed us sardines on toast, then put us into a large comfortable bed, so that in a second it was morning.

Whether we paid anything to get our bicycles over the barrier of the Trent I do not remember, but as I approach the bridge today I can't resist planning an attack on the toll collecting booth. I put the organisation into the hands of my old character Bill Straw who says: 'The police are tipped off, and they establish road blocks east and west to wait for us. But not to worry. They don't realise that our attack is going to be made from the *banks of the Trent*, north and south, and that there'll be a speed boat on the river for a quick getaway to Goole. Our lads will be disguised as gentlemen-hikers travelling the river. They'll have beards to hide the scars on their faces.'

I nod at his sagacity. A bearded bargee with a hand at the tiller floats by and wonders if I am mad.

'They come to this white gate,' Bill Straw continues, 'shin up the bank, and get over the fence. Police uniforms are hidden by their walking jackets. They've each got a flat cap, a whistle, and a walkie-talkie from Woolworth's in their natty little rucksacks. So it's all set. They barge into the middle of the road and stop the traffic. A couple more of our lads come up from the Scunthorpe direction. Using their walking sticks as pick handles, they smash into the toll booth and grab the takings.'

'It's as clumsy a bit of organisation as I've ever heard,' I tell him.

But he gives that 'England's last hope' kind of laugh. 'Don't kid yourself. This is going to be the classic set-piece attack. Foolproof. Nowt can go wrong. You can rely on my ex-SAS lads to pull it off. They was all born in Worksop, like me, and you can't have a better recommendation than that!'

What Bill Straw doesn't know is that one vital component in the plan has been overlooked, though what that is I can't be bothered to imagine as I go up the bank and through the white gate.

Pedestrians don't pay at the toll bridge, and I walk into Dunham, glad to put the river behind me for the night, even if only for a couple of hundred yards. The tobacconist's shop is open so I buy a packet of cigars, then ask if there's any place in the village which will put me up. He mentions Wilmot House nearby, and there I find that bed and breakfast is to be had for the usual rate of eight pounds. Jack and Margaret Hoist run the place like home from home, and after putting back numerous cups of tea I sample their ample table d'hôte.

If it looks like rain tomorrow I can set off anyway because at the first onset of the Flood I need only make for the nearest red kiosk and phone Jack Hoist, who has offered to fetch me back to the soothing stove-side of Wilmot House from anywhere along the route. He'll also meet me at Gainsborough when the day's walk is over, which means I can use my cushy billet as a base for two nights instead of one. We chat for a while in the kitchen, and Mr Hoist, who is a South Yorkshireman born in 1931, seems surprised to hear that I am three years older than him.

154

Power Lines

Under my feet no earthquake shatters the geology. Overhead, clouds form and unform, but the firmament never alters in its role of universal timekeeper and shepherd of the senses. The clock and the soil are in benign juxtaposition, and though the met office forecasts rain I set out for Gainsborough, fifteen miles away, because the pine cone in my pocket has not yet folded up entirely. With feet in good condition, except for a slight ache at the ankle, I'm supercharged for a fair day's stint along the steely kris of the Trent.

Vapour from the cooling towers of Cottam power station exits at an angle of forty-five degrees, making the letter B in semaphore, though B for what? I suppose those who complain at their presence would be the first to rush to the telephone if on putting down the light switch nothing happened. As far as I'm concerned, when God said let there be light he didn't keep his promise till he had made a power station, and radiating lines of pylons mean we no longer have to grub around with hot candlewax dripping on to our fingers.

Fishermen sit at little white posts, and a lark ascends with a melodiously sharp trill over the semi-canalised river. The land beyond is flat, and flat to the right, and seems to go on flat for ever. Cows like to take an interest in what goes on. But nothing goes on very much. There's emptiness in their eyes, and in their unresponding flanks as I pass close. They sit and look with a pleading kind of curiosity until I have gone by, half hoping I've come to lead them to some place where life is less boring. I almost feel sorry at leaving them to their fate.

The zipper of my posh jacket – relic of the South Downs Way, the Grand Canyon, and the Wadi Kelt in Israel – won't grip properly, so it's as well there's no rain. One of many woodcock scared along the way shoots up from the path like an aeroplane to do a half circle over the wheatfield. A garden seems the only way to get into Laneham village from the path. The house is half farm and half caravan park, and nobody stops me as I walk by the parlour window, though a man stares from the barn door. The lawn is so well clipped I almost tiptoe, but give him a half wave and close the gate properly.

Inside the church are the kneeling figures of Ellis Markham and

156

Jervase his son, who lived nearby. Ellis was a favourite of Queen Elizabeth I, and she commemorated him in a couplet:

> Gervase the Gentle, Stanhope the Stout,
> Markham the Lion and Sutton the Lout.

I wonder what skinhead antics Sutton indulged in to deserve such an epithet from the Virgin Queen.

Piston engines sound like a great bee, and I wave at the friendly aeroplane. Good to feel shadowed. One gets like that, with so much walking. A woman taking her dog for a walk says: 'It's cold this morning, isn't it. Or am I *nesh?*'

The old word is immediately understood, as being afraid of the cold. In spite of the telly, dialect doesn't seem to be dying out. Glad there's a wind to keep me cool, I answer that it certainly isn't warm. Her face is lined, but the skin is ruddy. She has short brown hair and grey eyes. I suppose she's something over forty – that uncertain age. She wears a heavy mackintosh and polished brown shoes, and a scarf around her neck which will come up over her head if the wind increases.

'Do you live in the village, then?'

She names a town ten miles away. 'I drive here because I like the river.'

I tell her so do I, and that I'm hiking to Gainsborough.

'A lovely walk,' she says.

I want to know more about her. Conjecture doesn't seem enough, or is too slow a process. If there was a coffee shop in sight I would suggest a cup: 'Do you remember that raffle ticket you bought three months ago? Well, you won first prize, which was to have coffee and cake with me. We've been looking for you all over the place!'

She has a sense of humour, and might have acquiesced. But in life we pass everyone by – except the chosen few, and fate alone decides who they are.

We go cheerfully on our ways. The Ferry Boat pub reminds me that there used to be seven ferries in this north county area, but only the toll bridge at Dunham now contributes to fraternisation between

157

the two counties. Any domestic intrigue, sexual hugger-mugger or adventurous burgling between one bank and the other must be severely cut down unless the participants have a car, or are strong swimmers.

Something small and dark flaps on the lane like a scrap of tar paper, a relic perhaps from a house burned down, and that the sky has relinquished for me to look at. I almost step on a bat, which isn't able to fly, so I bend for a closer look. Not wanting it to bite me from the vacuum of its panic and distress I decide to slide it on to my map and carry it to the grass, but the more I try to arrange such transport, the more it fights to keep away. The next lorry or tractor will crush it, or a stray dog (or cat) might harass it.

My legs stiffen with bending, but I get it on to the map, wingspread flapping between Sutton and Saxilby, and am about to achieve lift-off when if flops back on to the road. I curse, in a friendly fashion, but it slews about and refuses to co-operate. I hold the cold leathery little body in the middle of the map while I walk, or waddle rather, across the road. With misplaced valiance it struggles to get off, and when I block its retreat it nips the palm of my hand. Such ingratitude can only be laughed at, and I set it under a bush where it might survive.

Every day is different going down river, certainly more peaceful than the flow of a road through a town. The banks are the same, but a lot of water has poured in from recent rain. Beginning to sniff the sea, it broadens at the next bend, then narrows again, as if unwilling to be tugged from the safety of the land. But the unmistakable pull of the tide has it, a 'bore' which goes as far as Cromwell Lock, fifteen miles behind.

The Aegir comes this far, a dreaded and phenomenal wall of water charging up with the spring tides, followed by a series of waves known as whelps. Maybe it doesn't happen any more, the river being tamer now. George Eliot tells of the Aegir and the floods it caused in *The Mill on the Floss* – the Floss being the Trent, and St Ogg's, Gainsborough.

A rebel tree flourishes in the stream as if taunting others to come and enjoy the cool water, a tangle of branches high above the flow.

158

Such a navigational hazard must be tricky at night, though I suppose there are warnings which can't be seen from the shore.

The other side is all Lincolnshire, a foreign country as far as I'm concerned, except perhaps for Skegness which, a fair dip beyond the horizon, is fifty miles away on the coast. The peewit with its idiotic squeak is flying and circling over the pylons, afraid to cross the river.

A long island in the middle, not delineated on the map, is covered in trees and bushes from end to end. Smoke from barrel-like cooling towers near Cottam fumes lackadaisically into the sky, eight enormous pots set on a stove to boil water so that someone can have a shave. Who? Binoculars bring them close, but the 650-foot chimney which dominates the complex (finished in 1968) is still a mile off.

Power station waste foams from a spout and makes a swamp between the river and the raised footpath, and a long chute carries gravel from the workings into a waiting barge. I walk each bend of the river, make no chords and cut no corners. A two-stroke engine is angrier than that of the friendly Chipmunk, from a lone biker practising assiduously, but the embankment diverges and his noise is left behind. I'm the only pedestrian this morning, so there's no danger of the path becoming a trench or boggy waste as on some parts of the Pennine Way.

In a horseshoe dip of the river below the power station the long white *Mariana* launches its way upstream. Fosdyke Navigation Canal enters the river at Torksey Lock, a Roman waterway joining Witham and Trent, and deepened by Henry I, thus connecting Nottingham to the Wash. The remains of Torksey Castle make a stark picture.

The railway running up to the Torksey Bridge crosses my path. Thick vegetation grows along the bank, but I work leftwards and push through to the top. The sleepers have been pulled up, though it looks possible to reach Torksey on the other side of the river, if you have the nerve to step over slats of wood, with the fiercely flowing water a long drop below. If Nottinghamshire was over there I might try, but as it is Lincolnshire, and because the high barriers look like part of the Berlin Wall, I decide not to.

159

Near Barton Ferry

A cow shakes its calf from her teats to make sure it runs with her when I approach. If the river weren't restricted by high banks it would be twenty miles wide. The land is too flat to allow any freedom. Gentle hills that arise in Lincolnshire do not begin on my side until some miles away. There's hardly a vale any more. A long green barge carrying pyramids of gravel floats by the thistle fields.

Several motor boats put more life into the scene. Opposite are a number of storage gasometers, or maybe petro-chemical containers. Pancakes of cowcrap call for eyes down instead of on the eternal rope of water. Craft are cautioned to go dead slow for 450 yards. A cottage, visible for the last mile, turns out to be a heap of neat housebricks on one side, and on the other a sectional plan of the different rooms. A stove is still in place, a firegrate fixed, with two small water heaters and some cupboards – the one-time habitation of a shepherd or cowhand.

Views on the other bank are like pictures out at sea, but brought close as if by a mirage or optical illusion. A notice declares me to be in a private fishing area, by the grace of the Goole Angling Society, and I suppose they talk a lot among themselves with such an acronym! Trent Port with its sailless windmill, and the cemetery behind, is illuminated drastically by a shaft of sunlight against a background of bushes and trees. A tug called *British Waterways Robin Hood* goes by, instilling its presence on the placid water. A young man rows to a dredger, is hailed and hauled abroad – to cook what murky plan, I wonder.

No semblance of a track, I steer through deep grass from one white gate to another. The gates are double, one opens towards me, and the other has to be pushed out in front, a necessary system to stop cattle straying. At least I might have thought so, and maybe once it was, but there is no sign of a fence on either side. I have only to do a one-step left or right and go on my way, without opening and closing a gate twice to do so. Varying the monotony of my walk, I put on a Charlie Chaplin act and go through the gates, carefully closing each part behind me. Maybe the first step towards amusing others is to amuse oneself.

161

A score of black and white bullocks file down the embankment as if to cross my track. Are they going to give me a hard time? Each sturdy beast weighs at least twice as much as me, and stolid curiosity roots them to the track from which I have no intention of being detoured. I'm in no hurry, so talk to them, explain where I'm going, at which they listen as if my tale is too tall to be believed, or so banal as not worth considering. I can't tell which, but they step aside as I go forward.

When they follow I turn, and spin another yarn to stop them in their tracks. It works every time. The one who seems to be their leader shakes his head, blunted pizzle swaying in the breeze. I wonder if he's going to butt me, not out of malice (necessarily) but because he's more bored than any of the others, which is why he has become the leader.

I listen for the thump of hooves, but they follow at a walking pace. You'd better not come too far, I say, or you'll get sore feet. At the next gate they lose interest, knowing their territory. In any case we all come from the same place, and will undoubtedly go back there. We aren't such strangers.

The cups of the power station boileth over. I wrote a poem about it thirty years ago:

EXFILTRATION

Men stand fishing by the river bend
where sewers gush into prolix creation
and, telescoping in a high scramble,
reach the twin chimneys of the powerstation.

There the suburbs stop. A pit shaft sinks
from axles into earth and grinding wheels
whine against the sky. Dynamos
sing to the drumbeat of hydraulic heels.

Smoke elbows upwards and particles
of poison fall in atom order rain,

162

in a slow slant over box-encompassed fields
and woods weeping with theodolite pain.

Poles with marks and numbers, men with lodestone
lungs plane-table limb and lifeline
from pasture on to paper, while boots lift
and plunge to crush an extant celandine.

Surveyors spread triangulation
and coalmines stare as from creation's dome.
Clouds pile over pylons: while sheep and people
having no opinions, turn towards home.

A couple of goats and a Shetland pony graze in a garden at Littleborough, a quiet hamlet of red farms and pleasant houses. The church from a distance looks no bigger than a toy. It's a greystoned chapel, and is in fact the smallest in the county.

The *Hobo* from Hinckley, and a red gravel barge, stir up mud as they chug by, so that I can smell the water, an odour which varies according to the geological bed of the river. I recall the minor tributary of the Leen that flows through Old Radford (one of the many streams that look like the hairlines of a leaf on a physical map of the county) that gives a rank bouquet of mud when copiously filled after heavy rain that scraped against the rim of both banks, a smell so thick you could almost taste it between your lips.

A cliff bank with red soil showing between the trees in Lincolnshire is illuminated by a splash of the sun when the wind drops. The river turns blue, and leaves rustle with pleasure. Cows in the distance look at me looking at them through binoculars.

A gravel barge called *Leeds Magnetic* goes by. Two huge brown geldings graze among the bullocks, suggesting that the lion may well lie down with the lamb – in certain circumstances. The map, my only reading matter, says that the land to my left is the OUT INGS, and beyond is a ditch called MOTHER DRAIN. At midday, opposite Naith Hall, a muddy little stream goes tributarying into the Trent. Stepping stones get me close to the middle, and then I leap.

163

On turning a bend the choppy water breaks into white caps. The pump house and transformer of another Karnak of the Trent Valley gives light and comfort, and the cooling towers resemble chemical retorts, steam playing around their tops like the laboratory kit of whoever might hope – foolishly – to make a new man out of the old.

At two o'clock I lunch off the same black loaf and Polish sausage, plus two oranges. It's pleasant to linger by swiftly flowing water while wheat rustles in the fields that will give a bountiful harvest if the rain holds back. Distant grain elevators are monolithic vats of plenty for the lean years. The land is unpeopled, no sign of life, and because the daily stages of my walk are so short, I mindlessly sit when the mood takes me, seeing neither cows, barges nor people. The Trent flows quieter than the Don at Doncaster – though that's in Yorkshire.

Wide open spaces are an unbeatable specific for the soul, and if the river has any surprises it's only because every time I think it's going to rain the sun comes out. The wind blows strong enough to roll me off the embankment, but I spread my cape, use my pack for a pillow, and lie back for half an hour.

With a brimstone butterfly for company I hoist my kit and push on. A railway diverges before Gainsborough, one branch for Sheffield and the other line to Doncaster. I go down the embankment to the right of the bridge and under the arch nearest the river to avoid the mud.

A warehouse or grain container, with SPILLERS written on its massive wall, gives off a smell of roasted wheat. Or something does. A plaque says that the road bridge into town was widened in 1904.

Jack Hoist answers the telephone (it worked first time: thank you, Gainsborough!) and comes to fetch me as arranged, so that in half an hour I am being driven to my cosy room at Wilmot House in Dunham. My feet can rest, and I hope my ankle will ache less in the morning.

After a nap and a bath I have my supper in the living-room with half a dozen other men who have something to do with oil wells – perhaps the one I saw working south of Stockwith on my tour of the county by car.

164

Trentside House

I treat myself to a pint in the neighbouring pub, and read as I drink, and marvel that the amiability of people who know each other is a long way from the prison world of Norman Mailer's novel about Gary Gilmore.

Back in my room I listen to morse code on my communications receiver from Hamburg and Haifa, Murmansk and Montevideo, an aerial hanging out of the window. Or I get weather reports on the Gulf of Mexico and off Cape Hatteras, and in some weird way envy those who are out on such rough seas.

I begin to wonder whether I haven't missed my vocation, and think that perhaps I should have been a tramp, a gentleman tramp, of course, with a private income, but a tramp nonetheless, because I believe that I could wander happily around the country (and the world) for the rest of my life.

The line of tall old warehouses backing on to the river forms the waterfront of Gainsborough. A couple of steam tugs take on grain. A ship, called the *Argo C*, port of registration Rochester in Kent, is having its decks hosed. Gainsborough (or should I say *Grainsborough?*) is still an active port, but there's a feeling that the place used to be more prosperous.

It's an ideal day for walking, with high cloud and warm sun. Back on the Nottinghamshire bank, I leave the Trent Port Hotel behind, and notice that the tide must be coming in because the river seems to be flowing inland. The *Bulk Moon*, from Limassol in Cyprus, is being loaded. A direction-finding loop by the bridge suggests that the ship is above 1,600 tons and carries a wireless operator.

Cranes by the Old Shipyard are filling the *Maureen Ann* with scrap swarf which smells like the inside (and outside) of factories I worked at. The public footpath runs nearby, and I dodge a forklift truck, making my way between stacks of timber.

Cornfields are to my left, and an impenetrable band of bushes separates me from the river, but along the raised footpath hundreds of red poppies grow. Looking back at the boiling pots of the power

166

station, I almost expect to see a forlorn missionary inside, complete with topee, trying not to call on Man for help.

There's a sound of birds above wheatfields, the river visible through the trees. I cut off a bend because the area is overgrown, having no wish to tackle jungle. The path goes inland, as it were, over a bridge by a pumping station which spans a wide steepbanked dyke. Huge foxgloves stand among nettles as if on parade.

Walking for three days has made my body accustomed to its burden. Reality comes back, however, because my ankle aches, and I don't regret that only a few miles remain to the end of the walk. I suppose a gentleman tramp would rest for a couple of days in one of the many bed-and-breakfast havens conveniently placed around the countryside.

Blocks of straw are toppled all about in crazy sculpture, as if someone angrily made his way into the various parts of the haystack looking for the Golden Needle, which he didn't find. Otherwise nothing disturbs the peace, except the bray of a cockerel from Point Farm. Two seats have been put up by some good soul who at one time enjoyed the view of Walkeith, and the bend of the river going towards wooded hills.

Two brick structures belong nowhere, but must have been left from the war, though they are in good condition. One is a concrete building on which light ack-ack guns must have been placed, while the other served as an office or billet.

Peas are planted near the river, with poppies spotting the wheat beyond. At West Stockwith modern water cruisers languish in every other yard and garden. Perhaps having a boat is as important as possession of a car in these parts. A lock crosses the Chesterfield Canal where it joins the Trent, and from the high footpath I see the cruising launch *Trisantona II* go by. A forlorn boat among the thistles, with peeling black and white paint, seems even in too bad condition for me to consider buying.

A red admiral settles at my feet, so vividly and precisely coloured that it reminds me of those pictures on cigarette cards collected in childhood, one of the few examples in which nature is gaudier than

The Trent

art. A stench comes from somewhere, perhaps the stench of West Stockwith, from cabbage fields north of the village. Over the River Idle, the White Hart advertises pub grub and a beer garden.

When I came here last winter damp stains marked many cottage walls, and other dwellings were heaps of rain-sodden bricks. The place seemed somewhat decrepit. A character walking down the street looked like Magwitch from *Great Expectations*, but a Magwitch who had missed his moment of prosperity and glory.

I felt that the village had seen better days, though there was an air of something stirring nevertheless, of sprucing things up for when transients came to play with their seasonal cabin cruisers in the summer. The *Rob Job*, *Jackdaw* and *White Heather* were already waiting.

It's a nautical place, however, with an air of Dutch neatness about it. A helmsman's wheel rested on the wall of a nicely painted cottage near the telephone box, in one window the model of a ship in full sail, and a mass of tulips in the window below. In the garden a bucket swung from bare branches to frighten the birds, though there was nothing for them to eat. The sound of a mason's hammer came from behind a cottage that was being refurbished, but the impression was of damp, flat land that ate into all foundations.

East Stockwith, on the Lincolnshire side, looked sedate and clean, even a shade drier, as if it positively shunned the river, though I supposed that West Stockwith appeared equally remote and neat from that side.

Now it is summer, and everything is dry, bright and peaceful. The church of 1722 has huge windows, and inside a marble monument to William Huntington, a ship's carpenter, in whose memory and at whose expense the church was built. He also left money to many charities in the village. The life-size half-reclining figure wears waistcoat and boots, and is holding the drawing of a sailing ship.

Every house seems to have a barking dog behind the wall, or the door, or the window. Welcome to West Stockwith! The luxuriant flowers of prettily laid out gardens give off perfumed smells. The way beyond the village goes by cabbage fields, and after half a mile I get to the north-east point of the county. The river goes on its way to the Humber, twenty-two miles or another day's march away.

No particular features mark the boundary, only a cluster of houses called Heckdyke, so at a reference point on the map, at eleven o'clock, I sit on the low wall for a second breakfast. The land is flat as far as the eye can see, and saying goodbye to the river and the open sky, I turn on my tracks and walk down the main street of West Stockwith to look for a bus stop.

Eighty miles of my Trent Walk is finished, from Long Eaton to Heckdyke. One could follow it to the Humber, and do the whole thing comfortably in a week. I've indicated the possibility of an addition to the Long Distance Footpath system – if one dislikes hills and enjoys the sight of a river day after day. It's certainly a good way to feel Nottinghamshire soaking into your boots.

After little more than a mile I stand by a post, and a few minutes later mount the steps into an empty double-decker. For eighty pence I am taken back to Gainsborough, not directly, but through Misterton, Walkeringham and Beckingham, observing the local people getting on and off.